NIBBLES FOR BUBBLES

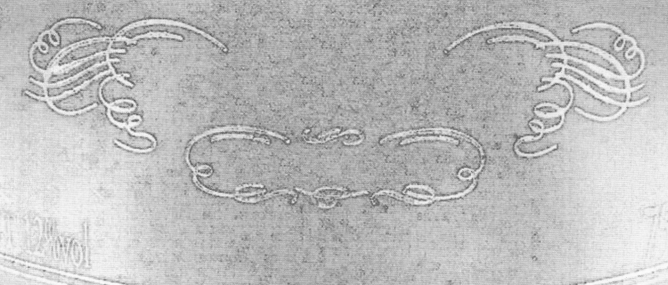

CONTENTS

INTRODUCTION

Canapés and amuse-bouches offer tiny tastes of one's favourite foods whilst lifting one's spirits with a glass of bubbles. They are perfect morsels to pop into your mouth when you have only one hand free!

Every culture has its encased treats of local flavours: sushi is a mainstay in Japan; the Chinese adore steamed or fried wonton parcels; Indians enjoy samosas and curry puffs; the French utilise crepés and fine pastry tartlets that explode with flavour; the Vietnamese wrap thin rice noodles, prawns and peppery mint leaf in rice paper and those from the Mediterranean use layers of fine filo pastry to hide savoury or sweet fillings. Meat filled enchiladas, or cheese and chilli quesadillas, are the taste bud teasers of Mexico. The British create delicious little sandwiches. What they all have in common is that element of surprise and delight when flavours, texture and tanatalising aromas are revealed.

Today we all travel widely and our palates are adventurous. Most of us love to eat food that triggers memories of special places we have visited and of the first time we tried local delicacies. In this book I want to share my private recipe collection gathered over the years of my various global roamings. I hope they evoke similar memories of your food journeys and inspire you to gather friends around to reminisce. Many are heirloom recipes which have been lovingly shared with me by generous friends and chefs. Some scribbled on scraps of paper no longer reveal the source.

All the recipes, however, are tried and true. I have prepared and served each and every one of them on both formal and casual occasions. They have been adapted, tested and fine-tuned to suit the most fastidious and the most basic of taste buds. You would be surprised how a plate of honey-glazed sausages can throw the sophisticate into a frenzy!

Canapés, or nibbles as I prefer to call them, do not have to be labour-intensive. Many items can be made well ahead of time. At home I am always prepared for the arrival of dear friends for a sundowner in the courtyard, a picnic in the park, or a lazy afternoon on board a boat. In my opinion there is never an inappropriate time to share these wee treats.

SOME PROFESSIONAL ADVICE

Entertaining is one of the great pleasures in life and a little thoughtful planning will ensure every occasion is a success. The ambiance you create and the ease at which you put your guests are equally as important as the food. Give great consideration to the temperature and time of year and keep the food fresh and refrigerated until serving time. Conversely, heartier fare and wafting oven smells set the tone on a wintry evening.

Before deciding on recipes, take into account the number of people, why they have been invited, your budget, whether you will have someone to help you, the amount of bench space, serving plates and glassware, and the most crucial – plenty of napkins.

Once you have these things sorted, the food will be easy!

START EARLY

Most nibbles can be prepared ahead of time. Blinis, pancakes, croutons, muffins and pastry tart cases freeze very well. Fillings and toppings can also be made the day before. The food has to be balanced and the guests should not leave hungry.

I would suggest 3-4 lighter nibbles before a sit-down dinner. A filled tart case can be popped into the oven while dinner is being prepared; a blini topped with a scallop or prawn is even easier.

For a 2 hour event when the guests are expected to disperse (and possibly go on to dinner) then about 8-10 canapés per person would be sufficient.

Should the event be longer, then cater for 10-12 nibbles per person finishing with a soup shot or something more substantial.

It is also important that you, too, enjoy the party and mingle with the guests. Consider hiring some service staff: a butler and a waitress per 25 guests can also help with plating and presentation. Otherwise delegate some duties to ensure there are no empty glasses, everyone has a nibble, and your stress levels are in check!

MAKE IT LOOK STYLISH

Presentation is important. Croutons and blinis offer a perfect canvas for your creativity. Consider a lovely plate which will show off the food but not distract from it. Fresh herbs and colourful edible flowers really lift a platter. If the guests are to help themselves from a buffet table then consider tiered cake stands which bring colour and interest to the table. Try not to overcrowd the dishes so that each 'nibble' has a chance at centre stage!

> ## ESSENTIAL INFORMATION
> As you go through this book you will see that I often use cup measures. The cup is a standard 250 ml measure. One cup of flour equals 150g.

MENU SUGGESTIONS

My recipes are an appetising collection to suit varying tastes and would suit most occasions. Be creative with your selection and combine tastes carefully. I have included some menus for specific events which I hope you will find useful.

Menu for 20 or more guests for 2-3 hours

Smoked salmon wrapped quail eggs
Herbed pancakes with duck in hoisin sauce
Blinis topped with smoked trout paté
Wild mushroom risotto cakes
Broccolini, blue cheese and pine nut tartlets
Caramelised beetroot and goats curd tartlets
Foie gras and Sauternes jelly on brioche toasts
Scallop with orange and ginger butter in spoons
Fennel and almond soup shots
Frangipane tarts

Menu for a self serve buffet table for 20 or more

Bagna cauda (garlic dip) with croutons and grissini
Asparagus spears wrapped in prosciutto
Herbed pancakes with duck and hoisin sauce
A selection of quiches and tarts such as wholemeal
    pumpkin and pine nut quiche, wild mushroom
    tarts or broccoli tarts
Thai chicken puddings or pork balls in hoisin
Nori wrapped prawns, with potato crisps and
    mango mayonnaise
Filo samosas or cheese and spinach filo
A selection of sweets such as coconut and lime curd
    filled aniseed pastry tartlets, petite peach and
    Ricotta cakes, frangipane tarts, or lemon posset
    garnished with a rosella flower.

Menu for an afternoon tea (champers) celebration

Cheese biscuit selection
Egg and caviar sandwiches
Goats cheese cakes
Lemon and dill blinis with smoked salmon
Orange and blueberry muffins with duck liver paté
Quail egg Scotch eggs or chicken and rocket sausage rolls
Carrot and leek tarts
Tamarillo upside down cakes, or sweet oven pancakes

"Champagne is
the only wine that
leaves a woman
beautiful after
drinking it."

Madame de
Pompadour

1

FAVOURITES

So here are some of my favourite canapés for large or small gatherings. They are a balance of fabulous flavours and textures but they are not complicated. With simple pre-planning and preparation you will avoid that eleventh hour panic - only a few of the delicate items require last minute grilling or cooking. I always like to have time to fuss over the final presentation and, if amongst friends, relax and enjoy their company.

I have selected recipes for foie gras and scallops to add a touch of luxury. I have a passion for seafood whether it be the whitebait fritters of my home country, cold water fish of the Atlantic, or the fresh prawns and scallops of Australia. I also have a strong liking for Asian food, and have added some delights for you to share.

Finally, I have included a frangipane mix - one of the most versatile recipes in my repertoire. It is ideal for that spontaneous sweet treat.

Enjoy sharing my favourite nibbles . . . and don't forget to have the bubbles close by.

GRILLED PROSCIUTTO WRAPPED ASPARAGUS SPEARS

Asparagus spears
Prosciutto, thinly sliced -
   1 slice per 2 spears
Olive oil
Parmesan, finely grated
Freshly ground black pepper

Trim the spears to the desired length - 10 -12 cm for a formal party. Wrap with the prosciutto and place on a baking tray. Drizzle with olive oil, grated Parmesan and season with black pepper. Place under a hot grill for just a few minutes.

SPINACH AND CHEESE FILOS (SPANAKOPITA)

500g frozen cooked spinach,
   thawed and drained
1 ½ tbsp freshly grated Parmesan
1 tsp olive oil
2 tbsp parsley
1 spring onion, finely chopped
½ tsp fennel seeds
75g Feta cheese
Pinch of nutmeg
½ cup cottage cheese
Salt and pepper
1 packet filo pastry
100g butter, melted

Preheat the oven to 180C. Mix together the filling ingredients. Work with one sheet of filo at a time and cover the remainder with a damp cloth to prevent it drying out. Brush the sheet with a little melted butter and fold in half lengthways and then in half again to form a long layered strip. Place a spoonful of the filling mixture at one end, then lift the right hand corner of the pastry to cover the filling. Continue folding in this way until a layered triangle is formed. Seal the end with a little butter and repeat to make more triangles. Place the pastry triangles on a greased baking tray, brush with a little extra butter and bake for about 15 minutes or until golden brown. **Makes about 36.**

BAGNA CAUDA (GARLIC DIP)

12 plump cloves garlic, skinned
Milk
30g butter, melted
7-9 anchovy fillets in oil, chopped
100ml olive oil
Truffle, optional
A variety of vegetable crudités,
   grissini or croutons

Place the garlic in a small pan and add just enough milk to cover the garlic cloves. Bring to a simmer and cook until the garlic is soft. The milk should gradually reduce in the time it takes for the garlic to become tender. Take care to avoid the milk catching on the bottom of the saucepan. Remove from the heat and allow to cool a little. Transfer to a small food processor. Add the anchovies and some of the oil. Process until smooth. Add the melted butter and oil gradually whilst continuing to process. Place in a small fondue dish with a small burner and add some grated truffle on top. Serve with crudités, grissini or croutons.

HERBED PANCAKES WITH DUCK IN HOISIN SAUCE

Herbed pancakes
250g (1 ⅔ cups) plain flour
60g butter, melted
250ml milk
250ml cold water
4 eggs
Salt and freshly ground black pepper
3 spring onions, finely chopped
1 cup fresh herbs, soft ones such as
    parsley, dill, coriander, mint, basil,
    chives and Vietnamese mint

Blend the flour, butter, milk, water and eggs until smooth. Refrigerate overnight. When ready to use add all the finely chopped herbs and spring onion. Add more cold water if the batter is too thick. Pour a thin layer into a medium hot greased blini pan to get the base evenly coated with the batter. When nicely tinged on the base, flip and cook on the other side. The pancakes roll more easily if warmed a little before filling and rolling. The pancakes freeze very well. **Makes 70 if made in a 10 cm blini pan.**

Duck filling
(enough to fill 35 pancakes)
1 large duck breast,
    trimmed of excess fat
1 ½ tbsp hoisin sauce
1 small tbsp sweet chilli sauce
2 spring onions, finely chopped
1 small carrot, finely julienned
    then diced
1 small bunch of coriander,
    finely chopped
2 tbsp mint, finely chopped
Crisp lettuce, finely shredded

Place the duck breast skin side down in a medium hot frying pan in order to release some of the fat. Do not burn. Drain the fat from the pan from time to time. Cook on the other side. Finish cooking in a medium to hot oven to save time. Allow to cool. Finely shred the duck breast and mix with the spring onion, carrot, coriander, mint, hoisin and chilli sauce. The mixture should be moist not wet. Place a small spoonful of the duck mixture and a little crisp lettuce in each pancake and roll. A dob of the sauce at the edge of the pancake will help seal it.

Variation: Make pancakes with:
80g buckwheat flour
40g plain flour
1 egg
280ml cold water
A pinch of salt and
1 tbsp vegetable oil

Mix all the ingredients together and rest for an hour or so before cooking. Thin the mixture with a little more water if necessary.

LEMON AND DILL BLINIS

150g (1 cup) self raising flour
1 egg
1 egg white
1 cup milk or 1 ¼ cups buttermilk*
1 tsp baking powder
Salt and freshly ground black pepper
1 tbsp fresh dill
Zest of 1 lemon
*For a more substantial blini use
     buttermilk

Mix the flour, whole egg, milk, baking powder, salt and pepper to form a fairly thick but dropping mixture. Add the dill and lemon zest. Whip the egg white to form a stiff peak and gently fold into the batter. Cook immediately in a heated, lightly oiled pan. A small teaspoon of mixture is sufficient for a cocktail blini. Top with smoked salmon roses or smoked trout mousse. Just before serving drizzle with a little lemon juice and black pepper and garnish with sour cream and dill. **Makes about 40 cocktail blinis.**

Oatmeal blini
125g fine oatmeal
125g bread flour
1 tsp salt
4g dried granular yeast
225ml warm milk
225ml warm water

Place the oatmeal and the flour into a bowl with the salt. Place the yeast in a little warm milk and water. Rest for about 30 minutes. Stir into the flour and oatmeal and add the remaining liquid. Cover the bowl and allow the mixture to rise for an hour or so. Cook as one would for blinis or pancakes in a greased pan.

Wholemeal blini
100g (⅔ cup) self raising flour
50g (⅓ cup) wholemeal plain flour
2 ½ tsp baking powder
1 whole egg
250-300ml milk or buttermilk
1 egg white, whisked till stiff
Salt and pepper
Herbs of choice depending upon
     the topping

Mix all the ingredients together except the whisked egg white which should be folded in just before cooking. Cook as per lemon and dill blinis above.

Variations to the blini mix
Add chopped prawns and corn to a blini made with buttermilk and serve with sweet chilli sauce.
Add wakame or arame seaweed to blini mix and top with whitebait.
Add some cooked wild rice to the blini mix and top with fried prawns and chilli jam.

Toppings
Smoked salmon, asparagus and citrus salad.
Smoked eel or tuna with beetroot relish.
Smoked trout mousse.
Marinate cucumber slices in rice wine vinegar, sugar and dill, place on a little mascarpone, and add smoked seafood.
Make a ball of mascarpone, wrap with smoked salmon, place on top of a cucumber slice and garnish with dill.
Diced smoked salmon with wasabi cream - 1 tbsp crème fraîche, a squeeze of wasabi paste and a pinch of sugar and squeeze of lemon juice.

ORANGE AND BLUEBERRY MUFFINS WITH DUCK LIVER PATÉ

½ cup caster sugar
⅓ cup butter
1 egg
½ tsp bicarbonate of soda
½ cup buttermilk
150g (1 cup) plain flour
Pinch of salt
¼ cup dried blueberries,
    cut in half
Zest and juice of ½ an orange
Duck liver pate or smoked
    duck fillet to serve
Sauternes jelly, or chilli jelly
    optional
Micro herbs to serve

Heat the oven to 190C and grease 4cm muffin tins. Cream the butter and the sugar until light and fluffy. Add the egg and beat well. Add the bicarbonate of soda to the buttermilk. Beat in the flour, salt, orange zest and a little orange juice into the buttermilk mixture. Mix into the creamed butter mixture. Add the blueberries. Spoon the mixture into greased mini muffin tins. Bake for about 12 minutes until golden. Cool on a rack. When ready to serve slice the top off each muffin and top with duck liver pate, or scoop a little of the centre out to make a dent and fill with rolls of finely sliced and rolled smoked duck fillet topped with pepper or chilli jelly or your favourite fruit jelly. **Makes about 50-60 cocktail muffins.**

WILD MUSHROOM RISOTTO CAKES TOPPED WITH PROSCIUTTO

50g butter
1 medium onion, finely chopped
250g mushrooms, finely chopped
2 cloves garlic, crushed
2 cups arborio rice
350ml dry white wine
1.5 litres chicken or vegetable stock
Zest of 1 lemon
⅓ cup flat leaf parsley,
    finely chopped
70g Parmesan, finely grated plus
    extra to garnish
Salt and pepper
Mayonnaise
Flat leaf parsley
Thinly sliced prosciutto
Parmesan shavings
Truffle oil

Use half the butter to fry the onion until soft. Add the mushrooms and garlic and cook until soft. In another pan heat the remaining butter and fry the rice until toasted. Add the onion mixture. Heat the wine and stock and add to the rice a ladleful at a time, stirring continuously until all the liquid has been absorbed, about 20 minutes. Add the lemon zest, parsley and Parmesan. Season to taste. Spoon the risotto onto a parchment lined shallow baking tray and smooth out to about 1 cm thickness. Set aside to cool, then freeze until required. Remove the risotto from the freezer and set aside at room temperature to defrost slightly before cutting into canapé or entree size portions. Fry on both sides in a little oil until nicely browned. If the risotto is a little moist put in a preheated 180C oven for about 10 minutes. When cool, top the risotto cakes with a little mayonnaise, parsley leaf, prosciutto and some Parmesan shavings and drizzle with truffle oil. **Makes about 60 or 70.**

Variation
Risotto cakes are also excellent made with finely diced roasted pumpkin. Garnish with mayonnaise, parsley, prosciutto and Parmesan shavings.

BROCCOLINI, BLUE CHEESE AND PINE NUT TARTLETS

1 small bunch broccolini,
    cooked al dente, drained
100g soft blue cheese
Toasted pine nuts
300ml cream
2 eggs
2 shallots, finely chopped and sautéed
Shortcrust tart cases
Parmesan, finely grated
Truffle oil

Mix the blue cheese, cream, eggs and shallots together. Place 4 pine nuts in the bottom of each tart case. Add the cream mixture and top with small sprigs of the broccolini. Sprinkle with a little finely grated Parmesan. Bake in a 180C preheated oven until the custard is set. Just before serving drizzle with the truffle oil.

PEARL BARLEY & PUMPKIN PATTIES WITH GRILLED RED PEPPER

100g barley, cooked by boiling in
    salted water
1 onion, finely chopped
1 clove garlic, crushed
1 tbsp olive oil plus a little extra
    for frying patties
120g pumpkin, finely diced
1 tbsp plain flour
Salt and pepper
1 tbsp flat leaf parsley, chopped
1 large red pepper
1 tbsp balsamic dressing
½ spring onion, finely chopped
    to garnish
Small chilli, finely chopped to garnish
Flat leaf parsley leaves to garnish
40g Pecorino cheese, finely grated,
    optional

Fry the onion and garlic in the olive oil until soft. Then fry the pumpkin until golden and soft, or roast in a 220C oven. Add to the onion and garlic. Add the cooked barley, flour and parsley and season. Roll into small balls and flatten into discs. Fry in a little oil. Dry out in a moderate oven for about 10 minutes. Cool. Cut the pepper into quarters and remove the seeds. Place under a hot grill until the skin blisters and is blackened. Cover with a clean tea towel and when cool remove the skin. Finely slice and add the balsamic dressing, spring onion and the desired amount of chilli. To assemble, place a leaf of parsley on the patty, top with the red pepper, spring onion, chilli and cheese. Makes about 16 x 4cm patties.

Variation
Dice and fry a medium aubergine instead of the pumpkin or a smaller aubergine and a little grated sweet potato.

CRAB AND SAFFRON TARTLETS

Petite shortcrust tart cases
250g white crabmeat
125ml double cream
1 whole egg
2 egg yolks
Small bunch chives, finely chopped
Pinch of saffron threads
Juice of 1 lemon
2 tbsp dry sherry
Pinch cayenne pepper
Salt and freshly ground black pepper

Mix the cream, egg and egg yolks, chives, saffron, lemon juice and sherry together. Season and mix in the crabmeat. Fill the tart cases and sprinkle with the cayenne pepper. Bake in a moderate oven until just firm.

CARAMELISED BEETROOT AND HOMEMADE GOATS CURD TARTLETS

Caramelised beetroot
3 large beetroot, peeled and finely diced
1 tbsp brown sugar
Dash of balsamic vinegar
Salt and pepper

Season and roast the diced beetroot with the sugar and vinegar. Allow to cool before using.

4.5 cm butter puff tart cases
Fresh basil leaves
Soft goats curd
Basil jelly, optional

To assemble, place a whole basil leaf in the base of each tart shell, top with the beetroot and a quenelle of goats curd.

Goats curd
1 litre goats milk
2 tsp rennet, lemon juice or
    apple cider vinegar

Heat the milk to 40C and add the rennet. Stir gently just to mix. Allow to stand for the curds to form. When cool transfer to a muslin cloth and hang to drain or place in a sieve. Drain for at least 24 hours.

INDIAN STYLE SWEET POTATO AND CORIANDER PASTRIES

Vegetable oil or ghee for frying
2 medium onions, finely chopped
3 cloves garlic, crushed
1 tbsp fresh, finely grated ginger
1 sweet potato, boiled whole
4 medium potatoes, boiled whole
1 chilli, finely chopped
1 tsp ground coriander
1 tsp garam masala
1 tsp cumin seeds
1 small bunch fresh coriander,
     finely chopped
Butter puff pastry sheets
1 egg yolk
Nigella seeds to garnish

Heat the oil in a frying pan and fry the onions, garlic and ginger until just cooked. Peel and finely dice the potatoes. Add with the spices to the onion mixture. Add the fresh coriander and mix well. Cut the puff pastry sheets into 6cm rounds and place a spoonful of the mixture into the centre. Fold the pastry over and pinch the edges together. Brush with the egg yolk and sprinkle with the nigella seeds. Bake in a 200C oven for about 20-30 minutes.

PORK BALLS IN HOISIN SAUCE

500g fine pork mince
1 tbsp garlic, crushed
2 tbsp ginger, finely grated
⅓ cup hoisin sauce
⅓ cup soy sauce
¼ cup sugar
¼ cup rice wine
¼ cup water chestnuts,
     finely chopped
¼ cup shrimp or prawns,
     finely chopped
Small bunch of coriander,
     finely chopped
1 egg white
2-3 cups good chicken stock
Crisp lettuce leaves cut into
     7 cm rounds, optional
Chopped spring onion to garnish
Toasted chopped peanuts for garnish

Combine the pork, garlic, ginger, hoisin sauce, soy, sugar, rice wine, water chestnuts, prawns, coriander and egg white in a bowl and refrigerate overnight. Roll into small balls. Bring the chicken stock to a simmer and add the pork balls a few at a time. Simmer for about 10 minutes. Serve in little crisp lettuce leaves or in Chinese spoons. Serve garnished with the chopped spring onions and peanuts. These pork balls have a deliciously soft texture and require care in the cooking process. **Makes 50.**

FOIE GRAS AND SAUTERNES JELLY

Foie gras
One fresh goose liver about 800g
1 cup good port
Dash of cognac
Salt and pepper

The liver must be at room temperature. Open up the liver and carefully remove any veins still present. Soak the liver in milk for a few hours. Drain and pat dry. Season the liver lightly and place in a China or glass bowl. Cover with the port and cognac and allow to marinate for 24 hours. Arrange the liver in a quart size terrine with a lid and cook in a bain-marie in a 180C preheated oven. Using a meat thermometer check that a core temperature of 75C is reached. Allow to rest in the terrine for 24 hours before turning out. Cut into 1 cm x 2cm x 3cm portions. Serve on brioche toast and top with Sauternes jelly balls.

Sauternes jelly
½ litre good chicken stock
1 egg white, lightly beaten
1 egg shell
1 tbsp gelatine
⅓ cup Sauternes

Bring the stock to a rolling boil. Add the egg white and the egg shell. Boil for about 5 minutes. Strain through muslin into a bowl. Add the gelatine and dissolve. Add the Sauternes. Either pour the cooled aspic onto the foie gras or make little balls by placing some clingfilm across the top of a small glass. Using your finger make a deep dent in the top of the clingfilm. Fill with the Sauternes jelly and bring the corners of the clingfilm together and twist to make a ball. Put in the refrigerator to set.

WHOLEMEAL BUTTERNUT PUMPKIN QUICHE

Wholemeal pastry
15g butter
1 small onion, finely chopped
1 small butternut, finely diced
300ml double cream
3 eggs
½ cup grated tasty cheese
1 tbsp chives, finely chopped
1 tbsp sage, finely chopped
100g pine nuts, toasted
Salt and pepper

Roll out the pastry and line mini muffin tins. Chill before filling. Sauté the onion and butternut in the butter. Combine the eggs, cream, cheese and herbs and mix well. Add the sautéed onion, sautéed pumpkin, and pine nuts. Fill the pastry cases and bake for about 30 minutes until pastry is cooked and the filling is set.

Variation
Pumpkin and spinach - add a cup or two of finely shredded spinach.

SCALLOPS WITH ORANGE AND GINGER BUTTER

8 large scallops in their shells
A knob of butter
2 cm piece fresh ginger, grated
Juice of 2 oranges
Juice of 1 lime
Juice of ½ lemon
1 tsp sugar
A little finely julienned fennel (optional)
Micro herbs, to garnish

Gently remove the scallops from their shells, trim and remove the roe. Clean the shells for presentation. Bring the juice and ginger to the boil and reduce by half. Add 1 tsp of sugar and set aside. In a hot frying pan heat a small amount of the butter and fry the scallops a few at a time. Do not overcook. Deglaze the pan with the citrus if the butter is not burnt. To serve, place the scallops back in the shell, drizzle with the orange sauce and garnish with micro herbs or fine julienne of fennel which has marinated in a little of the citrus juice.

PRAWN BISQUE

100g butter
1 clove garlic, crushed
2 onions, finely chopped
1 ½ kg prawn heads and shells
2 carrots, finely chopped
2 celery sticks, chopped
½ leek, finely chopped
½ cup brandy or cognac
3 tbsp tomato paste
750ml dry white wine
500ml cream

Heat the butter in a large saucepan and add the garlic, onions, prawn shells and heads and cook for about 5 minutes. Add the vegetables as well as the brandy or cognac and tomato paste and mix well. Add the wine and 750ml of water. Season. Simmer gently for several hours. Strain and discard the solids. Return the liquid to a fresh saucepan and add the cream. Bring back to the boil but allow to cool a little before serving.

THAI CHICKEN PUDDINGS

2 red peppers, seeded and finely diced
3 stalks of lemongrass, finely chopped
4 kaffir lime leaves, deveined, chopped
4 cloves garlic, crushed
50g red curry paste
4 tbsp fish sauce
400ml coconut milk
1 kg chicken breast, finely chopped
Fresh coriander to garnish
Thick coconut cream to garnish
Sweet chilli sauce to serve

Preheat the oven to 180C. Process the red peppers in a blender or food processor until smooth. Add the rest of the ingredients and blend until well mixed and smooth. Spoon into lightly oiled muffin tins. Make a dent in the top of each pudding and pipe in a small dollop of coconut cream and garnish with a coriander leaf. Bake for about 7 minutes at 180C. Serve warm with a sweet chilli dipping sauce. **Makes about 70 canapé size.**

FRANGIPANE TARTS

250g butter
150g (1 cup) plain flour
2 ½ cups icing sugar
1 ⅓ cups ground almonds
10 egg whites
Figs, pears or feijoas, finely diced
    or raspberries
20 x 9cm tart cases, or smaller

Melt the butter in a saucepan and cook until golden. Put the flour, icing sugar, ground almonds and strained butter into a bowl and stir. Add the egg whites and mix well. Cover and refrigerate overnight if possible. Preheat the oven to 180C. Combine the fruit with just enough frangipane mixture so that the fruit is well covered. Spoon into prepared tart cases or directly into greased patty tins. Bake for about 20 minutes or until golden brown. Serve with soft whipped cream. **Makes about 20 x 9cm tarts.**

Variations
Use ground pistachios instead of the ground almonds and add the zest of a lemon.
Use ground hazelnuts instead of the almonds, zest of an orange and frozen cranberries.
Use ground hazelnuts and apricots.

> **Note:** This is one of my staples and I always keep a supply of the mix in the freezer. The sugar content ensures it does not freeze solidly and small quantities can be removed as required. It can be used to top diced pear or raspberries in tart shells, mixed with berries in patty tins without the tart shells, or mixed with dried fruit and nuts to make biscuits.

LEMON POSSET WITH HIBISCUS FLOWERS

450ml whipping cream
125g caster sugar
60ml lemon or lime juice
hibiscus flowers, or berries

Bring the cream and sugar to a rolling boil and boil for about 3 minutes. Remove from the heat and cool slightly. Add the lemon juice. Cool for 10 minutes and pour into little glasses. Chill. Top with hibiscus flowers or berries.

"I only drink champagne when I'm happy and when I'm sad. Sometimes I drink it when I'm alone. When I have company I consider it obligatory. I trifle with it if I'm not in a hurry and drink it when I am, otherwise I never touch the stuff unless I am thirsty."

Lily Bollinger

Hôtel des Comtes de Champagne
et
Maison des Musiciens

Située au cœur du quartier marchand, la rue de Tambour était l'une des plus actives de la vieille ville. Elle conserve la plus ancienne maison bourgeoise de Reims (dite Hôtel des Comtes de Champagne), datant du Moyen Age : au rez-de-chaussée, des baies restituées lors d'une importante restauration après 1918 ont remplacé les boutiques. A côté se trouvait la Maison des Musiciens, dont le décor exceptionnel a pu être sauvé en 1918 (il se trouve désormais au musée Saint-Remi). Cinq statues du milieu du XIIIe siècle constituent un ensemble rare d'art laïc : quatre instrumentistes entourent un auditeur qui tenait jadis un faucon sur le poing, sans doute un riche propriétaire.

Old trading artery in the medieval city, this street holds the oldest middle class house in Reims (Hôtel des Comtes de Champagne), next to which stood the Musicians' House.

2

TASTES of the WORLD

Like many from an Antipodean background, my palate was brought to life through the food tastes of other cultures. When I first travelled to the Northern Hemisphere as a young girl I was exhilarated by the variety of ingredients and produce in countries like France and Italy. Vivid colours and flavours that tasted as delicious as they looked. My love affair with food and wine began then, and will remain with me forever.

Since that time I have been lucky enough to sip champagne in the four corners of the world. Each journey brings new taste experiences into my repertoire and I return with renewed fervour to recreate the dishes at home. I adore the Asian liking for small eats, the use of herbs and spices and the range of produce. I also love the depth and richness of Middle Eastern cuisines.

I hope you enjoy the cosmopolitan recipes I have chosen for this section.

BASIL SEED AND MINT TEA

100g caster sugar
A handful of mint leaves
1 stalk of lemongrass or small handful
    of lemon verbena leaves
1 tbsp basil seeds
Lemon or lime wedges
1 tsp brown sugar
1 litre soda water
Crushed ice to serve

Dissolve the caster sugar with ½ cup of water over a low heat. Add half the lemongrass or half the lemon verbena leaves to the hot sugar syrup. Stand for about an hour to infuse. Strain and chill. When ready to use cover the basil seeds with a little cold water for about 10 minutes for the seeds to swell. Strain, reserving the seeds. In a jug combine the lime, brown sugar, mint and rest of the lemon verbena if using, then add the basil seeds and sugar syrup, crushed ice and top with soda water.

VEGETARIAN RICE PAPER ROLLS

10 cloves garlic, crushed
1 cup vegetable oil
Rice paper wrappers

Add the garlic to the oil and heat over a medium heat. Cook until the garlic is golden. Strain.

Filling
6 coriander roots
5 cloves garlic, peeled
1 tsp ground white pepper
85g firm tofu, chopped
¼ carrot, chopped
8 dried shiitake mushrooms,
    soaked in water until soft
¼ cup green peas
1 tbsp sugar
2 tbsp light soy sauce
1 spring onion finely sliced on the
    diagonal to garnish

Crush the coriander roots, garlic and pepper to a paste. Fry paste in 2 tbsp garlic oil for 1-2 minutes until aromatic, then add tofu, carrot, mushrooms and peas and stir for 2 minutes. Add sugar and light soy sauce, stir, remove from heat and set aside to rest at room temperature. To assemble, place a spoonful of mixture onto each rice paper and roll. Garnish with spring onion and serve with the dipping sauce.

Dipping sauce
100ml dark soy sauce
250ml white vinegar
150ml light soy sauce
150g sugar
5 small red chillies, finely chopped

Combine all the ingredients in a saucepan over medium heat and stir until the sugar dissolves. Remove from heat and cool to room temperature.

PRAWN, CHICKEN AND WATER CHESTNUT DUMPLINGS

500ml chicken stock
2 chicken breasts
25ml fish sauce
15ml fresh lime juice, strained
40ml tamarind juice
2 tbsp mint leaves, chopped
1 tsp ground rice
200g raw prawns, chopped
1 tbsp water chestnuts, blanched, chopped
1 tbsp straw mushrooms, blanched, chopped
18 wonton wrappers

Poach the chicken breasts in the stock. Chop and blend in a food processor with fish sauce, lime juice, tamarind juice, mint, and ground rice until it resembles crumbs. Mix with the prawn meat, chestnuts, mushrooms and 1 tbsp coriander paste. Spoon a tsp of the mixture into the centre of each wrapper. Brush the edges with a little water. Pinch the edges together to enclose the filling. In small batches steam the dumplings for about 6 minutes or until cooked. Serve with dipping sauce. Makes 18.

Coriander paste
2 tsp garlic, crushed
½ tsp black peppercorns, freshly ground
A few Sichuan peppercorns, ground
3 coriander roots
25ml vegetable oil
2 tsp fish sauce
2 tsp strained lime juice
½ cup coriander leaves, chopped

In a food processor process all the ingredients into a smooth paste.

Dipping sauce
80ml light soy sauce
2 tbsp rice wine
2 tsp fresh ginger, grated
1 small fresh red chilli, seeded, finely chopped
2 tsp brown sugar

Mix all the ingredients together and serve with the dumplings.

COCONUT CHICKEN IN SESAME CUPS

500g chicken, skinned and diced into 2cm cubes
3 cloves garlic, crushed
60ml palm, cane or white vinegar
1 bay leaf
¼ tsp ground white pepper
Vegetable oil for frying
1 cup coconut milk
1 tbsp coconut cream powder
Chillies or herbs for garnishing
Sesame cups

In a bowl mix the garlic, vinegar, bay leaf and white pepper and add the chicken. Marinate for at least 30 minutes. In a pan heat the oil and fry the drained chicken pieces until brown and well sealed. Add the coconut milk and a little of the marinade and simmer for about 20 minutes over low heat until the chicken is tender and the liquid has nearly evaporated. Add the coconut powder and simmer for another couple of minutes. Serve in the sesame cups.

VIETNAMESE STYLE PRAWNS WITH MINT TIED WITH GARLIC CHIVES

Prawns, cooked, peeled and deveined
Vietnamese mint or herbs of choice
Garlic chives or regular chives

Tie the herbs to the prawn using the chives. Serve with a mint dipping sauce.

VIETNAMESE PANCAKES

250g rice flour
½ tsp turmeric
400ml coconut milk
Pinch of salt
4 spring onions, finely chopped
Oil for frying

Mix the rice flour, tumeric, coconut milk and salt to make a batter. Bring to a pouring consistency by adding water. Allow the mixture to stand for a couple of hours. When ready to cook add the spring onions. Heat and grease a 10cm blini pan and pour a thin stream of batter into it, tipping the pan to evenly coat the base. When the pancake begins to crisp around the edges add the pork, shrimps, onion and bean sprouts. Roll the pancake up and slip onto a plate. Serve with the fresh herbs.

Filling
½ onion, finely sliced
175g of shrimps, cooked and peeled
250g pork belly
250g bean sprouts, blanched
Vietnamese mint, basil, coriander
    leaves for garnish

Put the pork belly into salted boiling water and simmer for 15-20 minutes. Allow to cool. Slice thinly and set aside. Blanch the bean sprouts in boiling water.

PRAWNS WITH TAMARIND ROLLED IN RICE PAPER

16 large cooked king prawns, peeled,
    deveined and butterflied
A little lemon juice
3 tbsp sugar, plus 1 tbsp for dip
1 tbsp salt
4 red chillies, finely chopped
4 cloves garlic, finely chopped
50g tamarind pulp
2 tbsp fish sauce
4 tbsp roasted peanuts, crushed
16 sheets rice paper
1 bunch mint
1 Lebanese cucumber, julienned
1 cup bean sprouts

Squeeze a little lemon juice over the prepared prawns and set aside. In a food processor pulse the sugar, salt, chillies, garlic and tamarind pulp. To make the dip take 1 tbsp of the paste and mix with 1 tbsp sugar, fish sauce and 2 tbsp of the crushed peanuts. To assemble squeeze the juice from the prawns and place in a bowl with the remaining tamarind paste. Coat each prawn with the remaining paste and sprinkle with the remaining peanuts. Soften the rice paper sheets and place one prawn in the middle, add mint leaves, a piece of cucumber and some sprouts. Roll to form a tight roll and serve with the dipping sauce.

COCONUT AND GINGER PANCAKES WITH FIVE SPICE PORK

Coconut and ginger pancakes

80g rice flour
Pinch salt or dash of fish sauce
200ml coconut milk
1 egg
1 tbsp palm sugar
1 tsp grated ginger
2 tbsp plain flour
Coriander leaves, to garnish
1-2 tbsp peanut oil for frying

Mix together the first 6 ingredients to form a smooth paste. Thin with a little cold water if the mixture is too thick. Rest the mixture for at least a couple of hours. Lightly grease a 10cm blini pan evenly with the peanut oil. Place a coriander leaf in the base of the pan and pour the batter in a thin stream into the pan and tip the pan from side to side to cover the base. Flip and cook on the other side when the underneath starts to colour. If during cooking the mixture does not hold well then add some plain flour. Set aside to cool until ready to fill with the pork. The pancakes freeze well. **Makes about 20-25.**

Five spice pork filling

300g pork belly
330ml ginger beer or cider
1 tsp five spice powder
1 onion, finely sliced
3 cloves garlic
1 cucumber, julienned
1 carrot, julienned
1 spring onion, julienned

Place the onion and the garlic in a small baking dish. Add the five spice and place the pork on top. Add the ginger beer or cider. Cover the dish with foil and bake in a 150C oven for a couple of hours or until the pork can be separated with a fork. Allow to cool in the liquid. When ready to use finely shred. To assemble, cut the pancakes with an 8cm or 9cm pastry cutter if the edges are too rough for a formal party. Warm the pancakes a little so that they are easy to roll and place some shredded pork, cucumber, spring onion and carrot in the centre and roll.

Variation
Fill the pancake with chicken and mint.

SUZME ROLLED IN SUMAC, ZA'ATAR OR PISTACHIO

800g plain full fat yoghurt
200g goats curd -see recipe
100g hard goats cheese, finely grated
100g pistachios, finely chopped
2 tbsp za'atar
2 tbsp sumac
Dukkah

Place the yoghurt in a muslin cloth and stand in a sieve. Tie the muslin at the top, place over a bowl. Drain in the refrigerator for at least 24 hours. Prepare the goats curd. When ready to assemble place the suzme and goats curd and grated goats cheese in a bowl and combine until smooth. Shape the mixture into quenelles using two teaspoons and roll in either the finely chopped pistachios, za'atar, sumac or dukkah. Serve with Melba toast or warm bread or lavosh.

CHICKEN STUFFED LEMONGRASS

5 cloves garlic, crushed
4-6 medium spring onions,
    finely chopped
½ cup fresh coriander, finely chopped
1 kaffir lime leaf, deveined and
    finely shredded
1 tsp salt
200g chicken, beef or pork, minced
10-12 stalks of lemongrass,
    outside leaves removed
2 eggs, lightly beaten
Vegetable oil for frying

In a mortar and pestle or a blender pound the garlic, spring onions, coriander, kaffir lime leaf and salt. Add to the meat and mix well. With a sharp knife, and starting about 1cm from the base of the lemongrass, make a cut right through the stalk for about 4-5cm. Make sure to stop cutting short of the end so that the meat mixture will hold together. Make another one or two cuts in the lemongrass thus creating a central hole in which to hold the meat. Insert a spoonful of the meat mixture into the centre and shape with your hands. Dip into the beaten egg and fry in the oil until the meat is browned and cooked.

TANDOORI CHICKEN

2-3 chicken breasts, skin removed
150ml yoghurt
1 tbsp garlic, crushed
1 tbsp ginger, grated
1 chilli, finely chopped
Small bunch of coriander leaves
4 tbsp lemon juice
2 tsp garam masala
Salt
Red food colouring
Lemon slices to serve
Minted yoghurt to serve

Cut the chicken breast into bite size pieces. In a food processor blend the garlic, ginger, chillies and coriander together to make a fine paste. Add the other ingredients and marinate the chicken overnight. Skewer and grill or bake. Serve with slices of lemon and minted yoghurt.

MEXICAN CHICKEN

1 tbsp each paprika, oregano crushed,
    cumin, flour
1 tsp onion or garlic salt
2 tsp caster sugar
1 tsp chilli powder
Vegetable oil
8-10 chicken breast fillets

Mix all the spices together. Cut the chicken breast fillet into bite size pieces. Dip in the oil and then in the spice mixture. Grill or barbecue the chicken.

PRAWN TOASTS

350g raw peeled prawns
1 clove garlic
75g water chestnuts, chopped
1 tbsp coriander leaves, finely chopped
2 cm piece fresh ginger, grated
2 eggs, separated
½ tsp ground white pepper
¼ tsp salt
6-7 white bread slices
155g sesame seeds
Oil for frying
Sweet chilli sauce to serve

Combine the prawns, garlic, chestnuts, coriander, ginger, egg whites and salt and pepper in a food processor and process until the mixture is smooth. Cut small fingers from the bread slices. Brush each with lightly beaten egg yolk. Spread with the prawn mixture and sprinkle with the sesame seeds. Deep fry in batches until golden brown. Drain and serve with sweet chilli sauce or sweet and sour dipping sauce. **Makes about 30.**

INDONESIAN SPICED PEANUT BISCUITS

120g ground rice
1 cup coconut milk
1 tsp ground coriander
1 clove garlic, crushed
1 tbsp ground almonds
½ tsp salt
A pinch of cumin
250g unsalted peanuts, husks removed
Vegetable oil for frying

Mix all the ingredients together. Heat enough oil in a small frying pan to cover the base to about 10mm. The mixture should be thin enough to spread into a lacy wafer. Fry until golden. Drain on absorbent paper and serve sprinkled with sea salt.

SPRING ONION PANCAKES WITH SOY DIPPING SAUCE

450g (3 cups) plain flour
1 ½ cups boiling water
80g butter, softened
1 ½ tsp sea salt
2 bunches spring onions, finely chopped
About 80ml sesame oil
3 tbsp vegetable oil

Dip
80ml soy sauce
80ml rice wine vinegar
1 tsp sugar

Sift the flour into a bowl and stir in the boiling water. Knead dough on floured surface for 2-3 minutes. Cover the dough with plastic and let stand for 30 minutes. Divide into 6 equal balls. Roll each one out thinly. Spread 2 tsp butter over each circle of dough. Sprinkle with sea salt and spring onions. Drizzle with sesame oil. Roll up each pancake and arrange into a tight coil. Roll out again into a thin circle. Fry until crisp. Cut into wedges and serve hot with dipping sauce.

Mix until the sugar is dissolved.

MASALA DOSA

1 cup dhuli urad dal flour
2 ½ cups rice flour
½ tsp jeera seeds
Salt to taste

Potato filling
500g potatoes, peeled
2 medium onions, finely diced
2.5cm piece ginger, grated
1-2 chillies, finely chopped
¼ tsp turmeric powder
A couple of curry leaves
Salt
2 tbsp oil
1 tsp mustard seeds
¾ tsp urad dal
¾ tsp channa dal

Mix all the ingredients with salt and water to a thick consistency. Place in a warm place to ferment overnight. Dilute the batter with a little water until it stays thick but spreads evenly. Heat a thick based pan or a griddle and spread the batter evenly. Cook each side until the crust crackles and becomes golden. Fill whilst still warm.

Cut the potatoes into small dices and boil until just done. In a frying pan heat the oil and add the mustard seeds, the urad dal and channa dal. Add the onions, ginger, chilli and curry leaves. Sauté for a few minutes but do not brown the onions. Add the turmeric powder and potato. Season if necessary. Cook for a couple of minutes.

KANGAROO FILLET SATES

Kangaroo fillet
Sate sticks which have been soaked in
    cold water to prevent burning

Teriyaki marinade
½ cup soy sauce
½ cup sugar
½ cup medium dry sherry
1 tsp fresh ginger grated
2 garlic cloves, crushed

Variation
The marinade is also excellent
 with chicken fillet, lamb or
beef fillet as well as chicken
drumsticks and wings.

Cut the fillet into thin slices on the diagonal. Mix the marinade ingredients and marinate the meat for a couple of hours. Thread the meat onto sticks and barbecue.

Saté sauce
1 tbsp vegetable oil
1 clove garlic, crushed
1 small onion, finely diced
1 cup crunchy peanut butter
1 medium red chilli,
    deseeded and finely sliced
1 cup water
1 tbsp lemon juice
1 tbsp soy sauce
2 tsp brown sugar

Heat the oil and lightly fry the garlic and onion for 5 minutes without colouring. Add the remaining ingredients and simmer gently until thick. Set aside to keep warm.

TAKOYAKI (JAPANESE OCTOPUS (TAKO) BALLS)

A cast iron or electric takoyaki pan*
125g plain flour
320ml cup dashi soup
1 egg
125g boiled octopus,
    cut into bite-size pieces
¼ cup spring onion, finely chopped
1 tbsp pickled red ginger, finely chopped
Furikake seasoning
Mayonnaise to serve

Mix the flour, dashi soup and eggs in a bowl to make a batter. Grease a takoyaki pan and heat in a 220C oven. When hot place a little of the batter in the pan, top with the octopus, red ginger and spring onion. Sprinkle with the furikake seasoning. Return to the oven or cook under a hot grill flipping with a pick to turn. When browned, remove the balls from the pan and serve with mayonnaise.

*A griddle made of cast iron with half-spherical moulds similar to an old fashioned cast iron gem scone tray.

QUINOA SUSHI

1 cup mixed quinoa, cooked
3 sheets of nori
1 carrot, julienned
½ red pepper, thinly sliced
1 spring onion
1 small beetroot, peeled and julienned
¼ cup sesame seeds

Mix the dressing ingredients and pour over the cooked quinoa and combine well. Cover and rest for an hour or two. To assemble lay the nori sheets on a work surface. Spread the seasoned quinoa evenly over ¾ of each sheet. Arrange the carrot, spring onion, red pepper and beetroot in the middle. Roll the nori starting from the quinoa covered section and finish with the unfilled end. Seal the nori with a little water. Cut each roll into about 6 pieces.

Dressing
1 tbsp rice wine or cider vinegar
1 ½ tsp maple syrup
1 tbsp tahini
Juice of ½ lemon
1 tbsp grated ginger

Mix all the ingredients together.

NORI WRAPPED SOBA NOODLES

100g mixed soba noodles
2 nori sheets
1 carrot, finely julienned
1 spring onion, in long fine strips
1 tsp mirin
2 tbsp rice wine vinegar
1 tbsp tamari

Cook the noodles until just tender in salted water. Drain and rinse in cold water. Place 1 nori sheet on a dry work surface. Place a selection of noodles, carrot and spring onion onto one edge of the nori sheet and firmly roll. Seal the end edge with a little water. Cut into serving portions. Mix the mirin, rice wine vinegar and tamari together and serve as a dip.

STUFFED KIBBEH

450g lean lamb mince
Oil for deep frying

For the kibbeh
225g bulgur wheat
1 red chilli, roughly chopped
1 onion, finely diced
Salt and pepper

For the stuffing
1 onion, finely chopped
50g pine nuts
2 tbsp olive oil
1 ½ tsp ground allspice
4 tbsp chopped fresh coriander

Divide the meat into two portions. Soak the bulgur wheat for 15 minutes in cold water. Drain well, then process in a blender with the chilli, onion, and half the meat. Season well.

Fry the onion and pine nuts in the oil for 5 minutes. Add the allspice and remaining minced meat and fry gently breaking up the meat with a wooden spoon until browned. Stir in the coriander and a little seasoning. Turn the kibbeh mixture out onto a work surface and shape into a cake. Cut into 12 wedges. Flatten one piece in the palm of your hand and spoon a little stuffing into the centre. Bring the edges of the kibbeh up over the stuffing to enclose it. Make into a firm egg shape. Heat the oil to a depth of 5cm in a large pan. Fry for about 5 minutes.

PRAWN, CHILLI AND VIETNAMESE MINT DUMPLINGS

24 wonton wrappers
Peanut oil for frying
1 cup water

Filling
175g prawn meat, diced
1 small red chilli
8-10 sprigs Vietnamese mint,
    finely chopped
1 clove garlic, crushed
1 tsp fresh ginger, grated
1 tbsp sesame oil
1 tbsp light soy
Pinch black pepper
1 ½ tsp cornflour

Mix all the ingredients in a food processor. Place a teaspoon of mixture in each wonton wrapper. Brush the wontons with water and wrap around the mixture. Heat a little peanut oil in a frying pan, add the dumplings and brown on one side. Add the water or vegetable stock to the pan, cover and steam until cooked.

Dipping sauce
2 kaffir lime leaves , finely chopped
2 tbsp Japanese soy
2 tbsp black vinegar
2 tbsp fish sauce
Juice of 1 lemon
1 tbsp grated palm sugar

Mix all the ingredients together and serve with the dumplings.

EMPANADAS

1 ½ tbsp vegetable oil
1 small to medium onion,
    finely chopped
1 clove garlic, crushed
200g minced beef
½ tsp ground oregano
½ tsp ground coriander
½ tsp ground cumin
400g can diced tomatoes
2 tbsp raisins
6 pimento stuffed olives, chopped
2 hard boiled eggs, coarsely chopped
Salt
6 sheets ready rolled shortcrust pastry
A little milk to seal the pastry

Sauté the onion and garlic in the oil. Add the beef, oregano, spices, tomato and raisins and simmer for at least 20 minutes to reduce the liquid. Remove from the heat and cool a little before adding the olives and the eggs. Cut the pastry into rounds and place a spoonful of the mixture into the centre of each pastry round. Brush the edge with milk and fold the pastry in half and pinch the edges together. Place on a parchment paper lined baking tray and bake in a preheated 200C oven for about 15 minutes or until golden.

FILO SAMOSAS

1 tbsp ghee
1 clove garlic
1 tsp finely grated fresh ginger
2 medium onions, finely diced
2 tsp curry powder
½ tsp salt
1 tbsp malt vinegar
250g minced lamb or beef
1 tsp garam masala
2 tbsp chopped fresh coriander
Filo pastry
Melted butter for brushing

Heat the ghee in a saucepan over a medium heat. Cook the garlic, ginger and half of the chopped onion until soft. Add the curry powder, salt, vinegar and mince. Cook until the mince has browned. Add half a cup of water to the pan and cook until the meat is soft and all the moisture has been absorbed. Stir through the garam masala, coriander and the remaining chopped onion and allow to cool. Preheat the oven to 180C. Lay a sheet of filo pastry on the work surface (cover the rest of the filo with a damp cloth to prevent it from drying out). Brush the pastry with a little melted butter and fold in half lengthwise and then in half again to form a long layered strip. Place a heaped tablespoon of mince mixture at one end. Fold over the pastry to enclose the filling and brush with some melted butter. Repeat to make more filo parcels. Place the parcels on a parchment lined baking tray and bake for about10-15 minutes until the pastry is crisp and golden brown.

MOROCCAN STYLE QUAIL PASTRIES

2 quail or 1 spatchcock
1 tbsp butter
400ml chicken stock
1 onion, finely chopped
½ cinnamon stick
½ tsp ground ginger
Pinch of ground turmeric
1 tbsp fresh coriander, chopped
1 tbsp parsley, chopped
1 tsp caster sugar
A pinch of ground cinnamon
¼ cup roasted almonds,
    roughly chopped
Salt and pepper
¾ cup melted butter
1 tsp of orange blossom water
Brik pastry, spring roll pastry or
    filo pastry
Cinnamon and icing sugar to garnish

Brown the quail or spatchcock in the butter. Transfer to a casserole dish and add the chicken stock, onion, cinnamon stick, ginger and turmeric. Add extra water if the birds are not covered with liquid. Cook gently until cooked, about 1 hour. Allow to cool. Remove the birds from the stock and shred the meat from the bones discarding the skin. Remove the cinnamon stick and bring the stock to the boil and simmer until reduced to about ½ cup. Moisten the shredded quail with some of the stock. Add the chopped coriander and parsley. Mix the sugar, cinnamon and almonds together and add to the mixture. Season to taste. Add a drop of orange blossom water to the melted butter and brush the pastry sheets. Place a spoonful of quail mixture onto the pastry and roll into cigar shapes or make more substantial pastries for more than a nibble. Brush each with butter. Bake in a moderate oven till browned - about 10 minutes. Sprinkle with cinnamon and icing sugar.

TEMPURA QUAIL BREAST WITH KECAP MANIS DIP

Quail breast
½ cup rice flour
300ml chilled tempura batter
Vegetable oil for frying

Dust each breast lightly with the flour shaking off the excess. Dip into the tempura batter and deep fry until crisp and golden. Remove the quail from the oil with a slotted spoon, dry on absorbent paper and halve lengthwise on the diagonal. Serve with the soy dip or dishes of spiced salt.

Tempura batter
1 egg
100ml coconut milk
100ml soda water, chilled
150g plain flour
1 tsp salt

Mix all the ingredients together but do not over mix.

Kecap manis dip
50ml kecap manis
25ml light soy
25ml tamari

Mix all the ingredients together.

"Come quickly!
I'm tasting stars!"

Dom Pierre
Perignon, when he
first tasted his newly
created champagne.

Champagne

3

MORE THAN NIBBLES

Those guests who have managed to stand and chat for an hour or two will welcome something a little more substantial. They may even be lucky enough to find a chair and table and these slightly more robust recipes will be enthusiastically received. By that time, too, the alcohol may need to be mopped up!

I have selected a combination of recipes from light mousses and jellies to tarts, terrines and patés. Most can be made ahead of time. There is infinite choice and variety so let your imagination run wild.

GOATS CHEESE AND WILD GARLIC, CARAMELISED ONION OR BLACK GARLIC PITHIVIER

2 x 90g goats cheese rounds
3 sheets ready rolled butter puff pastry
1 small onion, finely sliced
1 egg yolk
2 tbsp pouring cream
4 sprigs wild garlic, garlic chives,
    finely chopped or black garlic cloves,
    halved

Sauté the onion until just cooked and not coloured. Add to the chopped wild garlic or garlic chives or black garlic. Cut discs the required size in the puff pastry. An ideal finger food size is to cut the base 6 cm and the top 8 cm. Mix the egg yolk with the cream and brush the base pastry. Slice the goats cheese and place on the pastry. Top with the herb and onion mixture. Cover with the larger piece of pastry and brush with the egg mixture. Crimp the edges with a fork. Place on a parchment lined baking tray and bake in a preheated 200C oven for about 15 minutes or until golden. Allow to cool a little before serving.

GROUSE DUMPLINGS WRAPPED IN PROSCIUTTO

200g pork sausage meat
100g grouse breast, minced
1 medium onion, finely chopped
1 clove garlic, crushed
2 tbsp parsley, finely chopped
6 juniper berries
50g pistachios
2 tbsp sherry or brandy
Finely sliced prosciutto
Croutons
Redcurrant jelly

Mix the sausage meat, grouse breast, onion, garlic, parsley, juniper berries, pistachios and liquor. Roll into balls and wrap with the prosciutto. Bake in a fairly hot oven until cooked. Serve on a crouton and top with redcurrant jelly.

Variation
Pheasant breast works well in this recipe.

BROCCOLI TARTS

1 sheet ready rolled puff pastry
1 bunch broccoli, cut into florets,
    blanched
2 tbsp olive oil
1 small onion, finely sliced
2 cloves garlic, crushed
Salt and pepper
60g Pecorino, grated

Line 11cm x 6cm shallow tins with the puff pastry. Sweat the onion and the garlic in the oil. Assemble the onion, garlic and broccoli on the pastry. Season. Sprinkle with Pecorino. Bake for about 15 minutes in a preheated 200C oven.

LOBSTER, PRAWN OR CRAB MOUSSE

500g cooked lobster, crab or prawn meat
300ml fish stock
100ml white wine
Dash of brandy (optional)
1 tbsp butter
1 tbsp plain flour
1 tbsp gelatine
½ cup fresh cream, whipped
Salt and pepper
1 tsp wasabi paste
Pinch of sugar
Prawn or chilli oil for garnish

Heat the fish stock, wine and brandy if using and add the gelatine to dissolve. Place half the fish stock mixture into a bowl and whisk in the wasabi paste. Pour a little into the base of 6 or 8 100ml ramekin dishes. Refrigerate until set. Melt the butter in a small saucepan, add the flour and cook for a minute. Add the remaining warm fish stock and gelatine and whisk until smooth. Cool. In a food processor blend the lobster, crab or prawn. Add the cool fish stock mixture. Transfer to a bowl and gently fold in the whipped cream. Season. Top the ramekins and allow to cool before turning out and serving. Drizzle the serving plate with a little prawn or chilli oil.

DUCK LIVER PATÉ

50g butter
500g duck livers
2 shallots, crushed
3 cloves garlic, crushed
1 ½ tbsp thyme, chopped
60ml brandy
60ml port
60ml Madeira
1 ½ tbsp Dijon mustard
325g butter, at room temperature

Soak the livers in warm water for an hour. Drain and clean. Melt a little of the butter in a frying pan over medium heat and fry the livers in batches until just cooked, wiping the pan between each batch. Add the garlic, shallots and thyme to the pan and sauté until transparent. Add the brandy, port and Madeira and flame to reduce to a syrupy consistency. Transfer to a blender and purée until smooth. Add the livers and mustard and blend until smooth. Add the butter gradually and season. Blend until smooth then pass through a sieve. Spoon into a large terrine and leave to set overnight.

PORK RILLETTES WITH PICKLED WALNUTS

1 kg skinned and boned pork belly
1 tbsp salt
3 bay leaves
3 sprigs of thyme
3 cloves garlic
1 cup dry white wine
Pickled walnuts to serve
Croutons to serve

Rub the pork with the salt and place in a roasting pan with the herbs and garlic. Add a cup of water, cover the dish with foil and place in a preheated 160C oven. Cook for 3 hours. Add a cup of dry white wine to the pan and cook for another hour until the pork is tender. Remove the meat from the juices then tear into fine shreds using a couple of forks. Pack into glass or China dishes. Strain the liquid from the pan and pour over the rillettes. Leave to cool then refrigerate. Serve with croutons and pickled walnuts.

GAZPACHO AND PRAWN JELLY TOPPED WITH SMOKED HADDOCK MOUSSE

2 cloves garlic
1 red pepper, cored and diced
1 large cucumber, peeled and diced
3 tbsp olive oil
1 green pepper, cored and diced
3 tbsp wine vinegar
1 small red onion, diced
400ml tomato juice or Clamato
5 large tomatoes
1 tsp paprika
Several sprigs of parsley
Salt and pepper
Small prawns or shrimps
3 tsp gelatine dissolved in 100ml warm
    water per 500ml of gazpacho
Smoked haddock mousse

Skin the tomatoes by plunging into boiling water and then into iced water. Blend in a blender or food processor with the remaining ingredients, reserving a little diced cucumber and parsley for garnish. Adjust the seasoning to taste. Strain off the liquid and add the gelatine. Place a couple of prawns at the bottom of shot glasses. Half fill the glasses with the gazpacho jelly and refrigerate until set. Top with smoked fish mousse and garnish.

TOMATO JELLIES WITH CRAB SALAD

Tomato jelly

1.5kg vine ripened tomatoes, chopped
2 shallots, roughly chopped
2 garlic cloves, crushed
1 cup tomato juice or Clamato
10 basil leaves, plus extra to garnish
2 tsp caster sugar
3 tsp gelatine dissolved in 100ml warm
    water per 500ml of tomato juice

Place the tomatoes, shallots, garlic, juice, basil, sugar and 1 tsp salt in a blender and whiz until finely chopped. Strain through a muslin cloth over a bowl. Do not squeeze as the juice will become cloudy. Reserve 100ml for the agar agar balls to garnish. Heat the remainder and set with gelatine. Half fill martini glasses.

Crab salad

1 tsp caster sugar
1 tbsp lemon infused olive oil
About 1 tbsp mandarin vinegar or
    juice of 1 lime
1 Lebanese cucumber, finely julienned
Micro herbs
200g fresh cooked crab meat
1 tbsp mint, finely chopped
1 long red chilli, finely chopped
Cherry tomatoes, skinned

Make the dressing by mixing the sugar, olive oil and the mandarin vinegar together. Mix the salad ingredients and add the dressing. Top the tomato jellies. Garnish with the agar agar balls.

Agar agar balls

100g tomato juice reserved
    from the jelly
1.5g agar agar
250ml oil

Place the oil in a tall glass and put into the freezer. Chill for about 1 hour. Add the agar agar to the tomato juice and bring to the boil. Remove from the heat and cool slightly. Using an eye dropper, or a syringe, drop the mix drop by drop into the chilled oil. Carefully remove the pearls from the oil using a fine sieve.

PORK, VEAL AND PISTACHIO TERRINE

4-5 rashers of bacon
750g pork and veal mince
250g chicken livers
2 onions, finely chopped
300g butter
2 cloves garlic, crushed
1 tbsp chopped parsley
3 eggs, lightly beaten
2 tsp salt
Pinch cloves or allspice
Pinch nutmeg
1 tsp thyme
Black pepper
½ cup port
½ cup pistachios

Line a terrine with the sliced bacon arranging the rashers so there are some to overlap the top of the dish. Clean and mince the chicken livers and mix in a bowl with the pork and veal mince. Sweat the onions and garlic in the butter and add to the meat along with the other ingredients. Mix well. Place in the terrine and overlap the bacon on the top. Place a piece of parchment paper on top then seal with foil. Cook in a bain-marie in a preheated 180C oven for about 2 hours. When cooked place a weight on top (about 1 kg) until the terrine is cool.

CHICKEN LIVER PATĒ GRAND MARNIER

250g chicken livers
Zest of ½ orange
1 tbsp butter
1 medium onion, finely chopped
1 tsp salt
3 tbsp Grand Marnier
½ tsp black pepper
½ tsp dry English mustard

Clean the livers. Sweat the onions in a little butter. Then cook the livers and orange zest in the foaming butter until the livers are just cooked. Process the livers in a food processor with the Grand Marnier, and mustard. Season. Press the mixture into individual ramekins or a clingfilm lined terrine. Top with the glaze and chill well before serving.

Glaze

1 tsp gelatine
200ml good chicken stock
Salt and pepper
1 tbsp Grand Marnier
Juice of ½ orange

Heat the chicken stock, stirring in the gelatine until dissolved. Add the orange juice and season. When off the heat stir in the Grand Marnier. Allow to cool before topping the paté.

MUSHROOM JELLIES

Mushroom Purée

2 tsp truffle butter
½ leek, white part only, finely chopped
200g white button mushrooms
100ml Noilly Prat
150ml chicken or vegetable stock
150ml double cream
Salt and freshly ground black pepper
3 tsp gelatine dissolved in 100ml
    warm water per 500ml of puréed
    mushrooms

Gently sauté the leek and the mushrooms in the truffle butter. Add the Noilly Prat, stock and cream and simmer for about 15 minutes. Remove from the heat and allow to cool a little. Purée in a blender until smooth. Dissolve the gelatine and add to the puréed mushrooms. Pour the mixture into the bottom of 6 glasses. Refrigerate and make sure the purée is well set before adding the jelly layer.

Mushroom jelly

500ml well flavoured homemade
    chicken stock
100ml dry sherry
200g mixed mushrooms
Salt and freshly ground black pepper
3 tsp gelatine dissolved in 100ml warm
    water per 500ml of liquid

Slice the mushrooms and simmer gently in the stock and the sherry. Season. Strain the liquid. To clarify drip through a jelly bag several times. When ready to use dissolve the gelatine and add to the liquid. Gently pour the jelly on top of the cream mushroom layer.

Sherry cream

100ml sherry
100ml double cream
Enoki mushrooms to garnish

Mix the cream and the sherry together and using a milk frother create a foam. Top the jellies and plant the enoki mushrooms.

PETITE CHICKEN AND SWEETCORN PIES

500g chicken breasts
1 tbsp olive oil
2 sweet corn cobs, cooked in salted water
50g butter
25g plain flour
375ml cream
2 tbsp parsley, finely chopped
1 tsp sea salt
Freshly ground black pepper
Ready rolled puff pastry
1 egg, lightly beaten, for glazing

Fry the chicken breasts in the olive oil, about 5 minutes on each side until cooked. When cool cut into small cubes. Set aside. Remove the corn from the cob and set aside. Melt the butter in a saucepan over a low heat. Add the flour and stir to combine. Cook for a couple of minutes without burning. Add the cream and simmer for a couple of minutes until thickened. Add the other ingredients and season. Line little pie dishes with the pastry. Fill with the chicken and corn mixture and top with the pastry. Glaze with the beaten egg and bake in a 200C oven until the pastry is cooked.

SLOW ROASTED TOMATO AND SHALLOT TART WITH BALSAMIC DRESSING

1kg cherry tomatoes
3-4 tbsp olive oil
200g shallots, peeled
2 cloves, garlic, crushed
Ready rolled butter puff pastry
Salt and pepper
6 thin slices prosciutto
Sprigs of fresh thyme
Mascarpone or goats curd
Balsamic dressing

Preheat the oven to around 75C. Dip the tomatoes into boiling water for a few seconds, then plunge them into iced water. Remove the skins. Place the skinned tomatoes onto a parchment lined baking tray. Brush with the olive oil and bake for a couple of hours to dry out slightly. In a frying pan brown the onions in a little oil. Add the garlic towards the end of cooking. Roll the prosciutto and crisp in the oven alongside the tomatoes. Line the tart tins with the puff pastry and bake blind. When ready to serve line the base with mascarpone or goats curd and place the tomatoes and onions on top. Warm in the oven. Drizzle with the balsamic dressing, top with the prosciutto and garnish with fresh thyme sprigs.

LAOTIAN STEAMED SALMON WITH DILL AND KAFFIR LIME

80g ground rice
2 cloves garlic, crushed
3-4 red chillies, finely chopped
2 stems lemongrass, finely chopped
100g spring onion, finely chopped
300ml coconut milk
2 tbsp fish sauce
2 tsp palm sugar
8 stems dill, chopped
8 kaffir lime leaves, finely chopped
400g salmon fillet, cubed
Banana leaves

In a blender process the garlic, chillies, lemongrass and spring onion with the coconut milk, fish sauce and sugar. Add the ground rice and mix. Allow the mixture to rest for at least 1 hour. Add the dill and kaffir lime leaves. Fold the banana leaves into the ramekins then add the salmon and pour the coconut mixture over the salmon. Steam for about 15 minutes and garnish with dill.

ZUCCHINI FLOWERS STUFFED WITH COD MOUSSE

20 zucchini flowers

Gently separate the petals and remove the stamen from each flower.

Cod mousse
200g cod or other firm white fish,
    chilled
200ml double cream, chilled
Salt and pepper

Roughly chop the fish and place in the chilled bowl of a food processor and process to a paste. Add half the cream and pulse, then add the remainder of the cream and pulse just to incorporate. Season. Transfer the mixture to a piping bag and pipe into each flower. Dip into tempura batter and deep fry. Serve with a saffron mayonnaise.

Tempura batter
Oil for frying

Saffron mayonnaise
½ cup good mayonnaise
1 tbsp Noilly Prat
A few saffron threads

Mix all the ingredients together.

MOROCCAN PRAWNS WITH COUSCOUS

1 tbsp light olive oil
7 cloves garlic, crushed
Zest and juice of a lemon
1 tbsp smoked paprika
2 small red chillies, deseeded and
    finely chopped
1 tsp salt
1 bunch flat leaf parsley, finely chopped
1 tbsp melted butter
8 large raw prawns, with shells on
1 cup coconut milk
250g small raw peeled prawns, deveined
Parsley to garnish
Lemon wedges to serve
Cooked couscous to serve

Sweat the garlic in the olive oil. Add the lemon zest and juice, paprika, chillies, salt and parsley and mix well. Divide the mixture in half and in one lot add the melted butter. Season. Remove the legs from the large prawns leaving on the head and tail. Make a slit on the underside and stuff with the butter infused mixture. Refrigerate until ready to cook. Barbecue or grill. Heat the coconut milk with the extra parsley mixture, add the small shelled prawns and heat until the prawns are cooked. Serve with couscous. Garnish with parsley and lemon wedges.

NOODLE BOXES WITH SEAFOOD AND RISONI IN A SAMBUCA SAUCE

500g mixed seafood - scallops, prawns,
    salmon or smoked fish fillets,
    mussels etc
2 small fennel bulbs
1 leek
600ml prawn or seafood stock
300ml cream
300ml dry white wine
1 tbsp Sambuca
1 tbsp butter
100g risoni, cooked in salted water
    (squid ink risoni or black rice
    is also excellent)
2 spring onions, finely sliced
1 tbsp capers, rinsed
Dill to garnish

Trim the fish and peel the prawns if using. Trim the leek and save the white part. Chop the top and put in a saucepan with the top of the fennel bulbs and stock. Simmer gently for an hour. Strain and add the cream and wine. Simmer to reduce to half. Add the Sambuca. Thicken with a little rice flour if still too thin. Finely slice the white part of the leek and the fennel. Gently sauté in the butter. Fry the fish and add to the sauce. Add the other seafood, the leek and fennel and spring onions. Just before serving add the capers. Garnish with the dill.

TERRINE OF LEEKS, TRUFFLE AND SOLE

6 medium leeks, white part only
2 truffles - 6 thin slices,
    the rest coarsely chopped
450g fillet of sole
200g trimmed scallops
2 egg whites
2 tsp salt
1 ½ tsp freshly ground white pepper
¼ tsp grated nutmeg
1 ½ cups chilled whipping cream

Cut the leeks in half lengthwise and blanch. Line the terrine with the blanched leeks. Finely chop the remainder of the leeks. Process the sole, scallops, egg whites, salt, pepper and nutmeg in a processor until quite fine. With the motor running add the chilled cream until it is thoroughly absorbed. Fold in the chopped leeks. Put a third of the mixture in the terrine, smooth the top and sprinkle with half of the chopped truffles. Layer with another third of the mixture and sprinkle with the remainder of the truffles. Finish with the remaining mixture. Fold the leeks over the top to enclose the fish. Cover with parchment paper then cover with foil. Poach in a bain-marie in a preheated 180C oven for about 1 hour. Cool, then refrigerate overnight. Slice and serve with fresh tomato sauce.

Fresh tomato sauce
8 large ripe tomatoes
⅓ cup chives, finely chopped
2 tbsp olive oil
1 tbsp tomato paste
Salt and freshly ground black pepper

Peel the tomatoes by blanching in hot water. Deseed and blend with the remaining ingredients.

SOLE MOUSSE WITH LOBSTER AND TRUFFLE, BROAD BEAN SAUCE

Lobster stuffing

50g lobster meat, cut into strips
2 large button mushrooms,
    finely julienned
20g butter
2 slices of truffle, cut into strips
1 tbsp brandy
2 tbsp double cream
Salt and freshly ground pepper

Sauté the mushrooms in the butter then stir in the lobster and truffle. Add the brandy and set it alight and then add the cream. Reduce slightly so the mixture combines together. Season and cool.

Sole mousse

200g fillet of sole, skinned and deboned
200ml double cream, chilled
Salt and cayenne pepper

Place the fillets with a pinch of salt in a food processor. Purée. Add half the cream and mix gently. Pass the mixture through a sieve into a bowl. Place the bowl over iced water and gently fold in the remainder of the cream, little by little. Season with salt and cayenne. Pipe the mousse into four buttered moulds, making a small hollow in the centre for the stuffing. Spoon the stuffing in the centre. Top with mousse. Cover the moulds with parchment paper and foil. Poach in a bain-marie in a preheated 180C oven for about 20 minutes or steam.

Broad bean sauce

200ml fish stock
100ml dry white wine
50ml Noilly Prat
1 small shallot, finely chopped
150ml double cream
50g butter, well chilled
Salt and freshly ground black pepper
100g broad beans, cooked and peeled -
    reserving a few to garnish

In a saucepan bring to the boil the fish stock, wine, Noilly Prat and reduce by half by rapid boiling. Add the cream and boil gently to reduce to the required consistency. Remove from the pan and whisk in the butter cubes, piece by piece. Season and bring back to the boil with the broad beans. Simmer for about 5 minutes. Liquidise and sieve.

> *"Maybe I misjudged Stromberg. Any man who drinks Dom Perignon '52 can't be all bad."*
>
> *James Bond*

4

BREADCASES & CROUTONS: RISOTTO & RÖSTI

The smell of fresh bread, the waft of baked goodies as they exit the oven, or the warmth of a perfectly cooked risotto. A dinner party menu? No, the basis of a sophisticated cocktail party. These seemingly basic staples can be transformed very easily into scrumptious nibbles. Whether it be breadcases to hold an array of delicious fillings, or croutons with special toppings, they each allow the cook to be creative with what else is available in the pantry or the refrigerator. Similarly, a risotto cake, rösti, scone loaf or muffin can provide the perfect canvas for the host to showcase his, or her, artistic flair.

A great excuse to go over the top with some foie gras, caviar or prized grouse.

DILL SCONES

300g (2 cups) self raising flour
1 tsp baking powder
2 tsp caster sugar
¼ cup dill, chopped
60g cold butter, chopped
⅔ cup buttermilk
1 egg, lightly beaten
Milk for brushing
Sea salt for sprinkling
Smoked salmon paté
Smoked salmon roe to serve
Sour cream to serve, optional

Blend the flour, baking powder, sugar, dill and butter together. Gently fold in the buttermilk and egg. Place the mixture into mini muffin tins, brush the top with milk and sprinkle with sea salt. Bake in a preheated 150C oven for about 10 minutes. Serve with smoked salmon paté and salmon roe.

BREAST OF GROUSE WITH REDCURRANT JELLY IN A BREADCASE

Prepared breadcases
Flat leaf parsley leaves
Cooked grouse breast, finely sliced
Bread sauce
Potato crisps, halved
Redcurrant jelly

Line a breadcase with flat leaf parsley. Add a little bread sauce. Arrange some slices of grouse breast and garnish with redcurrant jelly. Finish off with half a potato crisp. An excellent way to use up leftovers from a meal of grouse.

HERBED SCONES

3 heaped cups (500g) plain flour
2 heaped tsp cream of tartar
2 heaped tsp bicarbonate of soda
450ml full cream milk
150ml cream
200g diced savoury ingredients, such as
    sun-dried tomatoes, feta cheese,
    olives, slow roasted onions,
    Cheddar cheese, herbs of choice
Sweet chilli sauce for glazing

Sift the flour, cream of tartar and baking soda into a large bowl. Add the tomato, herbs, cheese, milk and cream and gently mix together. Do not over mix. Turn out onto a lightly floured surface and gently finish working the dough together. Lightly press down into small loaf tins which have been lined with parchment paper. Glaze with sweet chilli sauce. Bake at 150C for 25-30 minutes or until golden and cooked in the centre. Remove from the oven and allow to cool before cutting.

PARMESAN AND TRUFFLE BUTTER

125g butter at room temperature
80g Parmesan cheese, finely grated
20ml truffle oil
1 tsp lemon juice
2-3 tsp truffle paté or truffle sauce

Place the butter and the cheese in a food processor and blend. Add the truffle oil and the lemon juice. Gently fold in the truffle paté by hand, otherwise the butter will become grey. Refrigerate until ready to use.

SUN-DRIED TOMATO BUTTER

100g butter
1 ½ tbsp sun-dried tomatoes,
    finely chopped
1 chopped garlic clove, crushed
1 tbsp fresh basil, finely chopped

Place the butter, sun-dried tomatoes and garlic in a food processor and blend until smooth. Fold in the basil. Refrigerate until ready to use.

ROASTED RED PEPPER BUTTER

100g butter, softened
1 red pepper
1 spring onion, white part only,
    finely chopped

Cut the pepper in half and deseed. Place under a hot grill skin side up to blacken. Cover with a tea towel and remove the skin when cool. Place in a food processor and process with the butter until smooth. Blend in the spring onion. Refrigerate until ready to use.

WELSH RAREBIT TOPPED WITH BEETROOT RELISH

3 tbsp white wine or beer
100g Cheddar cheese
1 tsp dry English mustard
2 egg yolks
Salt and pepper or cayenne pepper
1 tsp Worcestershire sauce, optional
12 breadcases
Parsley or chives to garnish

Heat the wine or beer, Cheddar and mustard in a saucepan until the cheese is melted. Season. Beat in the egg yolks and Worcestershire sauce. Place a spoonful of the mixture in each breadcase and bake for a couple of minutes until golden. Top with relish. Garnish with parsley or chives.
Enough for 12.

Variation
Use thinly sliced white bread trimmed of the crusts. Place some mixture at one end and roll the bread to form a roll. Place on a parchment lined baking tray with the seam underneath. Grill until golden.

Beetroot relish
1 tbsp olive oil
1 shallot, finely chopped
1 tsp fresh ginger
½ tsp ground cardamom
1 large beetroot, peeled and
    finely grated
¼ cooking apple, peeled and
    finely grated
Juice of 1 orange

Gently fry the shallot. Add the other ingredients and cook gently for about 20 minutes.

BACON AND HERB LOAF

2 eggs
70ml olive oil
70ml milk
120g plain flour, sifted
80g grated Gruyere or Cheddar
1 tsp baking powder
Salt and pepper
Herbs of choice
Bacon or shredded prosciutto

Lightly beat the eggs with the oil and the milk. Add the flour, cheese, bacon or prosciutto and herbs. Season and stir. Add the baking powder. Pour into parchment lined mini loaf tins. Bake in a preheated 180C oven. Cool slightly before turning out.

SAFFRON FRENCH TOAST WITH SMOKED SALMON AND SALMON ROE

12 slices of brioche
2 eggs
125 ml milk
½ tsp saffron strands
30g unsalted butter
2 tbsp olive oil
125g crème fraîche
100g smoked salmon
Salmon roe to serve

Cut the brioche into 3cm rounds. Mix the eggs and the milk in a bowl and whisk. Add the saffron and set aside for an hour. Heat the butter and oil in a frying pan over a medium heat. Dip the brioche rounds in the egg mixture. Drain off the excess and fry for 1-2 minutes on each side. If the toasts are too moist, dry out in a preheated 140C oven. Garnish the toast with crème fraiche, smoked salmon and salmon roe.

BRIOCHE TOASTS WITH GOATS CHEESE AND HAZELNUTS

1 brioche loaf
Hazelnut oil
Creamy goats curd or cheese
Chopped roasted hazelnuts
Chives for garnish
Onion marmalade to garnish, optional

Slice the brioche into medium slices and cut out 4cm rounds. Brush with the hazelnut oil and dry out in a very slow oven. When cool, pipe with soft goats curd and garnish with chives, roasted hazelnuts and onion marmalade. This is a simple but delicious canapé.

MARINATED SARDINES WITH CUMIN, PEPPERY BREADCRUMBS AND FINGER LIME

75g stale ciabatta or sourdough coarse
   crumbs
1 tbsp mixed herbs such as thyme,
   oregano and rosemary
½ tsp coarsely ground black pepper
½ tsp sea salt
2 tbsp olive oil or oil from the
   marinated sardines
Knob of butter
1 clove garlic, crushed
Zest of a lemon
2 tsp cumin seeds
Marinated sardines
Finger lime beads to garnish

Heat the oil and the butter in a frying pan until foaming. Mix the breadcrumbs, herbs, and salt. Add the garlic to the foaming butter then add the crumb mix and fry until golden and crisp. Drain on paper towel. Add the lemon zest and cumin seeds if using. To assemble curl a sardine fillet and place in a Chinese spoon. Top with the fried crumbs and garnish with the finger lime beads.

Variation
Serve the sardines on toasted ciabatta or sour dough.

TOPPINGS FOR CROUTONS, CROSTINI, CROUSTADES ETC

To make croutons/crostini

Slice a baguette into thin slices. Butter them on both sides or brush with olive oil and rub with garlic. Fry in a hot pan or cook under a grill until crisp and golden.

Foccacia

Tunisian aubergine salad, and a quenelle of drained yoghurt.
Rare fillet of venison on garlic focaccia with jelly and parsnip crisps or with fried chestnuts and rowan jelly.

Seed bread

Mushroom, Brie and pine nuts.
Celeriac remoulade, ocean trout and fennel crisps.
Scrambled egg, mayonnaise and asparagus.
Soft boiled quail egg and wild mushrooms.
Roasted pumpkin, prosciutto, mustard and mayonnaise dressing and basil.
Quail breast and roasted red pepper in orange and hoisin sauce.
Quail breast with chestnuts and quince.
Venison fillet and celeriac remoulade.

Brioche

Roasted beetroot and celeriac remoulade.
Blue cheese, parsley and honey walnuts.
Wild mushroom, truffle sauce and pine nut.

Mayonnaise, ocean trout and asparagus.
Chicken liver paté, pepper jelly and grape.
Micro herb, scrambled egg and caviar.
Smoked tomato mayonnaise, baby bocconcini and slow roasted tomato.
Prosciutto, toasted aubergine, zucchini and roasted garlic.

Hazelnut oil brioche Croute

Goats curd and roasted hazelnuts.
Cream chevré, hazelnuts and red onion marmalade.

Bacon and corn scone loaf

Mozzarella stuffed pepper with bacon rind crisps.
Smoked tomato mayonnaise, roasted aubergine and zucchini with stuffed olive and rocket.

Pumpernickel

60g cream cheese, 8 green peppercorns, dash Pernod, cayenne pepper, 1 tsp horseradish, 1 tbsp cream and a squeeze of lemon juice mixed together. Spread on bread, top with salmon rose, finish with caviar and dill.

Olive bread

Goats cheese, walnut and grape.

Croutons/crostini

Vitello tonnato with baby capers.
Roasted butternut, Gorgonzola and sage.
Scrambled eggs, truffle and truffle oil.
Broad bean, prosciutto and Ricotta.

Anchovy topping

100g anchovy fillets, drained
2 garlic cloves, crushed
1 tsp tomato paste
1 ½ tbsp olive oil
2 tsp lemon juice
Black pepper
10 slices French bread, seeded loaf or focaccia
Chopped parsley to garnish

Blend together the anchovies, garlic and tomato paste. Drizzle in the oil a little at a time until the mixture becomes thick. Stir in the lemon juice and freshly ground black pepper. Under a grill toast the bread on one side. While still warm spread the anchovy paste on the uncooked side. Grill for a couple of minutes. Garnish with the chopped parsley.

Anchovy and walnut topping

4 anchovy fillets
75g walnuts
1 tsp lemon juice
2 tsp parsley, finely chopped
1 clove garlic, crushed
75g cream cheese
Salt and pepper

Blend the ingredients except the cream cheese which should be added last. Refrigerate before using.

PARSNIP RÖSTI TOPPED WITH SOFT BOILED QUAIL EGG, SMOKED EEL AND SAMPHIRE

1 medium onion, finely diced
250g parsnips, finely grated
1 medium potato, finely grated
10g butter
4 tbsp olive oil
1 egg
2 tbsp plain flour
Smoked eel
Soft boiled quail eggs
Samphire for garnishing

Melt the butter and oil in a pan and fry the onion. Squeeze as much moisture as possible from the grated parsnip and potato and add the onion mixture. Add the flour and the egg and mix well. Roll into patties and fry. Allow to cool before topping with smoked eel, soft boiled quail egg and samphire.

Variation

Celeriac also makes an excellent rösti topped with smoked eel and Sambuca mayonnaise.
Beetroot does also - top with soft quail egg and smoked haddock.
Sweet potato rösti is excellent with crispy duck and chilli jam.

MARINATED BREAST OF QUAIL ON PARSNIP OR CELERIAC RÖSTI WITH ALMOND MISO

Parsnip or celeriac rösti as above
6 quail breasts
Noodle salad dressing (dashi, light soy, Japanese vinegar, sugar and sesame oil)
Parsnip or celeriac crisp to garnish
Almond miso

Marinate the quail breasts for 1-2 hours. Drain and pan fry, skin side first, until the skin is crisp and the meat is slightly pink. Garnish the rösti with a parsley leaf, top with the quail breast, finish with the parsnip or celeriac crisp and almond miso.

SWEET POTATO AND WAKAME SEAWEED RÖSTI TOPPED WITH SMOKED TROUT

2 cups floury potato, grated
2 cups sweet potato, grated
2 tbsp wakame seaweed
Salt and pepper
½ cup plain flour
2 spring onions, finely chopped
1 egg
Mayonnaise
Smoked trout and nori to garnish

Mix all the rösti ingredients together. Roll into small balls and flatten before frying. Top with a dollop of mayonnaise, smoked trout and garnish with small pieces of nori.

FENNEL RISOTTO CAKES TOPPED WITH PRAWNS AND ANISE MAYONNAISE

1 large bulb fennel, finely diced
1 large onion, finely diced
3 garlic cloves, crushed
2 tbsp oil
500g arborio rice
1 litre fish or prawn stock
Salt and pepper
250g small prawns, peeled and deveined
1 persimmon finely julienned
Anise mayonnaise
Dill to garnish

Sweat the fennel, onion and garlic in the oil. Do not brown. Add the rice and cook in the oil for a couple of minutes. Slowly add the stock until the rice is just cooked. Add extra water if necessary. Season. Place the mixture onto a parchment lined baking tray. Smooth out evenly and chill, then freeze for a couple of hours. Cut with a 4.5cm cutter and fry on each side. If the rice cakes are still too moist place them in a preheated 180C oven for about 10 minutes. Top with a little finely julienned persimmon, a prawn, a dollop of anise mayonnaise and finish with a sprig of dill.

Anise mayonnaise
3 tbsp good quality mayonnaise
A splash or two of Sambuca or Pernod
1 tbsp sour cream, optional

Mix all the ingredients together.

COCONUT RISOTTO CAKES TOPPED WITH DUCK BREAST AND SHIITAKE MUSHROOMS

1 ½ cups arborio rice
1 medium onion, finely diced
2 stalks lemongrass, finely chopped
1 ½ cups chicken stock
1 ½ cups coconut milk
Duck breast, cooked
Shiitake mushrooms
Oil for frying

Prepare the risotto (as in Fennel recipe above) and top with duck and fried shiitake mushrooms.

POTATO CRISPS WITH TROUT PATÉ

2 trout fillets, skinned and deboned
1 ½ tbsp sour cream
2 tsp dill
Wasabi paste or horseradish
Squeeze lemon juice
Salt and freshly ground black pepper
Small potatoes
Oil for frying

Blend the paté ingredients together. Season. Chill before using. Finely slice the potatoes and deep fry until crisp. Sandwich together with the trout paté.

Variation
These crisps are also excellent with salt cod or smoked salmon paté.

BEER PANCAKES

125ml milk
50g butter, melted
150g (1 cup) plain flour
2 tsp oil
2 eggs
175ml beer
Several slices of diced smoked
    bacon, or the same quantity of
    smoked ham

Mix the milk, butter, flour, oil and the eggs. Add the beer and rest the mixture for several hours before cooking. Thin the mixture with milk if too thick. It should be the consistency of pouring cream. Add the cooked bacon or ham and pour a thin layer into a medium hot greased blini pan to get the base evenly coated with the batter. When nicely tinged on the base flip and cook on the other side. The pancakes freeze very well.

Variation
Eliminate the bacon and serve plain with berries and cream.

SMOKED CHICKEN IN MADEIRA JELLY ON POTATO CROUTON WITH CARAMELISED FIG

1 smoked chicken breast
½ pint good chicken stock
1 tbsp Madeira
15g gelatine
Egg whites for clarifying
Potato croutons
Caramelised figs to garnish
Parsley leaf to garnish

Trim the chicken breast of skin and dark edges and shred finely. Add trimmings (except the skin) to the stock and gently simmer. Strain and return to the pan. Reduce to 300 ml. Whisk the egg whites to form soft peaks. Spoon into the stock and simmer until clarified. Pass through a muslin cloth. Add the Madeira and the dissolved gelatine to the stock. Put the shredded chicken into a 10cm x 15cm flat dish lined with clingfilm and pour over the jelly. Allow to set. Using a cutter cut the chicken to the desired size, place on top of the potato and garnish with fig and a parsley leaf.

CHORIZO CORN PUPS

½ cup plain flour
½ cup cornmeal
½ tsp sugar
½ tsp baking powder
½ tsp salt
½ tsp chilli powder
1 egg
½ cup milk
2 tbsp vegetable oil
Peanut oil for frying
20cm chorizo cut into rings
Mustard or mustard mayonnaise
    for dipping

Mix the flour, cornmeal, sugar, baking powder, salt and chilli powder together. Mix the egg, milk and vegetable oil together and add to the dry ingredients. Heat the peanut oil. Put the chorizo rounds onto a stick, dip into the batter and fry in small batches. Serve with mustard or a mustard mayonnaise.

Variation
Also good with prawns or lobster.

BITTEBALLEN

A wonderful recipe which I helped two Dutch Michelin-starred chefs prepare for Queen Beatrix of Holland during her visit to Sydney.

1 cup of medium thick white sauce
1 tsp of gelatine
2 cups of chopped cold meat
    (chicken/ham)
1 tbsp parsley
1 tbsp hot pepper sauce (optional)

2 eggs mixed with a little milk
Breadcrumbs
Mustard and mayonnaise dip to serve

While the white sauce is still warm add the gelatine which has been dissolved in a little hot water. When cool mix all the ingredients and roll into small balls. Chill overnight. Dip the balls into the egg mixture then the breadcrumbs. Deep fry until golden. Make sure the balls are well coated with the egg and crumbs as when cooked the inside becomes lovely and moist. Serve with a mustard mayonnaise dip.

POTATO CAKES

500g floury potatoes
3 eggs, beaten
50g self raising flour
2 egg whites, whisked to soft peaks
½ cup hot milk
Salt and freshly ground black pepper
Butter or oil for frying

Boil the potatoes until soft, drain well and mash. In a large bowl mix the eggs, flour and potato then mix in the milk and season. Gently fold in the egg white. Shape into patties and cook in a greased frying pan over a medium heat. Top with any topping.

TARTE FLAMBÉ

250g unbleached white bread flour,
      plus extra for dusting
1 tsp fresh yeast
1 tsp golden caster sugar
1 tbsp olive oil
2 tsp salt

Topping
Crème fraîche
½ red onion, very thinly sliced
200g smoked streaky bacon, cut into
      thick pieces
100g Reblochon cheese, thinly sliced,
      Pont-l'Evêque, Brie or Port Salut

Mix 50g of the flour in a bowl with the yeast, sugar, 1 tbsp oil and 4 tbsp warm water. Leave for an hour in a warm place until the mixture is bubbly and doubled in size. Place the mixture in a food processor and with the machine running gradually add the remaining flour and the salt. Add about 2 tbsp of water to make a soft, but not sticky, dough. Roll the dough out thinly and cut into the desired size and shapes. Place on a parchment lined baking tray, spread the dough with the crème fraîche followed by the onions and bacon, making sure the toppings go to the edge of the dough. Season well with black pepper. Bake in a preheated 200C oven for about 20 minutes or until the tart is golden and the base is crisp. Top with the cheese and put back into the oven for a further 3 minutes or until the cheese has melted.

POLENTA FRITTERS TOPPED WITH SMOKY CHERRY TOMATOES

250ml milk
1 tbsp caster sugar
210g polenta
50g plain flour
80g Pecorino, finely grated
Vegetable oil for deep frying
Cherry tomatoes
Liquid smoke flavour*
Basil leaves to garnish
Mayonnaise to garnish

*Available in good delis

Bring the milk to the boil with 250ml water, the sugar and ½ tsp salt. Combine the polenta and the flour then gradually whisk into the milk mixture. Whisk until thick, about 1 minute. Remove from the heat and add the Pecorino. Cool slightly then roll the mixture into 2cm diameter logs. Cut each log into 1cm slices, then using your fingers, roughly indent each slice. Place on a parchment paper lined baking tray and leave to cool completely. Deep fry the fritters in small batches for about 1minute until golden. Drain on paper towel and season. Serve with smoky slow roasted tomato and a basil leaf. To make the tomatoes blanch them in boiling water then plunge into iced water. Peel. In a bowl toss them with a little smoke flavour and season. Drain and place on a parchment lined baking tray and dry out in a 50C oven for several hours. When cool place a little mayonnaise on the polenta fritter, add a basil leaf then a cherry tomato.

MUFFINS WITH TEA MARINATED QUAIL

¾ cup polenta
½ cup plain flour
1 heaped tbsp caster sugar
½ tbsp baking powder
1 tsp salt
¾ cup milk
¼ cup melted butter
1 egg, lightly beaten
Micro herbs to garnish
Chilli jelly

Preheat the oven to 190C and grease 4cm muffin tins. Combine the polenta, flour, sugar, baking powder and salt in a bowl. Mix the milk, butter and eggs together and stir into the polenta mixture until just combined. Add a little extra milk if the mixture is too thick. Spoon the batter into the greased muffin tins and bake for about 12 minutes or until golden. Cool on a rack. When ready to serve, slice the muffins in half and spread with the jelly. Add the micro salad and then the finely sliced quail breast.

Quail marinade

10g loose Lapsang Souchong tea
5g smoked or regular sea salt
2 tsp honey
Splash of Chinese rice wine or brandy
200g quail breast (readily available in
　　Australia)

Mix the tea, salt, honey and rice wine together. Marinate the quail breast in the mixture overnight. When ready to cook wipe the marinade from the quail and gently cook in a little oil in a frying pan. Be careful not to burn. When cool slice quite finely and fill the muffins.

OLIVE AND SUN-DRIED TOMATO MUFFINS

2 eggs
70ml olive oil
70ml milk
120g plain flour
70g hard cheese - Parmesan or Cheddar
1 tsp baking powder
Salt and pepper
100g sun-dried tomatoes, chopped
100g pitted black olives, sliced
Herbs of choice – chives, basil or parsley

Mix together the eggs, oil and milk and add the flour, cheese, tomatoes, a small quantity of the olives (reserving most for topping the muffins), seasoning and chosen herbs. Do not over mix. Add the baking powder and fill parchment lined and lightly greased muffin tins. Garnish with slices of olive. Bake for about 15 minutes. Cool in the muffin tray before turning out. **Makes 40 petite 4.5 x 2.5 x 1 cm muffins.**

MINI YORKSHIRE PUDDINGS FILLED WITH BEEF OR VENISON FILLET

110g plain flour
2 eggs
300ml milk
10g butter, melted
Sunflower oil or lard for greasing the tins
Fillet of beef or venison, cooked medium rare
Horseradish or rowan jelly
Rocket, flat leaf parsley or micro salad

Sieve the flour into a bowl. Add the eggs, milk and butter and mix well. Allow to stand for at least an hour before using. Preheat the oven to 230C. Generously grease mini muffin tins and heat the tins in the oven. When hot, half fill with the batter. Cook until puffed and golden. Allow to cool before filling with salad leaves and topping with finely sliced beef or venison fillet. Finish with horseradish or jelly.

CORN HUSK CHEESE AND BACON MUFFINS

Corn husks, blanched in hot water
1 tbsp vegetable oil
350g smoked streaky bacon, diced
2 spring onions, finely chopped
115g Cheddar cheese
300g polenta
350g plain flour
1 tbsp caster sugar
1 tsp baking powder
½ tsp bicarbonate of soda
½ tsp salt
375ml buttermilk
2 eggs, lightly beaten
½ tsp ground black pepper
2 tbsp butter, melted

Preheat the oven to 200C. Line the muffin tins with the soft corn husks. Cook the bacon in the oil. Add the spring onions and cook for five minutes. Remove from the heat and allow to cool slightly. Combine the polenta, flour, sugar and baking powder, bicarbonate of soda and salt. Add the bacon mixture, cheese, buttermilk and eggs, black pepper and the melted butter. Mix well but do not over mix. Pour into the corn husk lined tins and bake for about 20-25 minutes. Serve warm.

"I only drink champagne on two occasions: when I'm in love and when I'm not."

Coco Chanel

5

SEAFOOD & OTHER DELICACIES OF THE DEEP

Seafood is the most seductive of all fresh produce. It is what we choose when we want to make an impact, or to welcome friends from across the globe. For me there is no more perfect marriage than Champagne and a platter of oysters and succulent lobster and prawns. Australia and New Zealand are both blessed with abundant seafood from their surrounding pristine coastal waters, so I have been very spoiled over the years.

Most of these recipes, however, are designed to provide the guests with the same seafood treats, but in much more manageable form. Not easy to peel a prawn while holding both a social conversation and a glass!

MEXICAN PRAWNS

Brioche toast
4 tbsp melted butter
200g cooked peeled prawns
½ tsp chilli powder
¼ tsp paprika
¼ tsp cumin
Salt and pepper
Watercress to garnish

Melt the butter and add the spices. Add the prawns and heat through. Spoon on top of the brioche toast and garnish with the watercress.

MEXICAN FISH CAKES

450g firm white fish fillets
2 cloves garlic, crushed
2 tsp Mexican chilli powder
⅓ cup finely chopped fresh coriander
1 small chilli, deseeded and chopped
1 egg
½ tsp black pepper
1 tbsp lemon juice
2 tbsp chopped spring onions
1 tsp ground cumin
Corn husks

Mix all the ingredients in a food processor. Roll into sausage shapes. Wrap in corn husks and cook on a barbecue.

SESAME CRUSTED PRAWNS

1 egg yolk
Salt
½ cup black sesame seeds
½ cup white sesame seeds
Prawns, shelled with tails retained
    and deveined
Vegetable oil for frying

Beat the egg yolk with the salt. Mix the sesame seeds. Dip the prawns in the egg mixture then in the sesame seeds and deep fry.

QUENELLE OF SMOKED HADDOCK MOUSSE WITH LUMPFISH ROE

400g fillet of smoked haddock,
    skinned & deboned
50g carrot, peeled and finely diced
50g onion, finely chopped
50g celery, finely chopped
1 bay leaf
A few sprigs of parsley
A few white peppercorns
1 ½ leaves of gelatine, softened in cold
    water and squeezed dry
Juice of 1 lemon
240ml double cream
1 tbsp lumpfish roe
Pinch cayenne pepper
Salt and freshly ground pepper

In a small pot of water add the carrot, onion, celery, herbs and peppercorns and simmer for about 10 minutes. Poach the haddock for about 7 minutes. Remove and flake the fillet. Continue boiling the liquid and reduce to about 125ml. Add the gelatine and mix till dissolved. Strain. Blend the fish with the liquid until smooth. Season with the freshly ground pepper, cayenne, lemon juice and salt. Lightly whip the cream and fold into the fish. Pour into a container and leave in the refrigerator until set. Make a quenelle with hot spoons. Cut in half and spread the cut surface with the lumpfish roe. Serve with Melba toast.

Variation
Make the mousse with smoked salmon or smoked trout.

SALT AND PEPPER FISH WITH ORANGE AND WASABI SAUCE

750g diced white fish
2 tbsp rice flour
1 tbsp Sichuan pepper, ground
2 tsp sea salt flakes
1 tsp black pepper, ground
A knob of butter
A little oil for frying
A drop of orange water

Mix the rice flour and spices together and coat the fish with the seasoned flour. Fry in butter, oil and a drop of orange water.

Wasabi sauce
Juice of 2 oranges
1 onion, finely diced
1 tsp wasabi paste or to taste
A knob of butter

Place the diced onion in the orange juice and steep for an hour. Strain and discard onion. Reduce the orange juice by half by boiling. Add the wasabi paste and adjust to your liking. Whisk in a knob of butter.

MUSSELS WITH BASIL AND COCONUT

8 medium spring onions, finely chopped
1 stalk lemongrass, finely chopped
3 garlic cloves, crushed
2.5 cm piece fresh ginger, grated
2 tbsp vegetable oil
2 tsp shrimp paste
Touch of fresh chilli
Salt and pepper
3 eggs
2 tsp cornflour
¾ cup coconut milk
3 dozen basil leaves
3 dozen green lipped mussels

Blend spring onions, garlic, ginger and lemongrass to a fine paste. Heat oil in a wok. Add shrimp paste, chilli and spring onion paste and sauté until mixture is brown and the oil separates. Remove from the heat. Beat coconut milk, eggs and cornflour. Blend into the shrimp paste mixture and season. Free the mussels from the shell and place a basil leaf underneath each mussel. Cover the mussels with the sauce. Bake for about 10 minutes at 190C. Reduce the temperature to 180C and continue cooking until the sauce is set. Serve warm.

SMOKED MUSSEL AND SWEET POTATO FRITTERS

2 tbsp plain flour
1 tsp baking powder
Salt and freshly ground black pepper
1 egg yolk
Water
250g smoked mussels, chopped
½ cup kumara (New Zealand sweet
    potato), grated
1 tbsp chopped chives or spring onions
A little oil for frying

Place the flour and baking powder into a mixing bowl and mix in the egg yolk and water until it forms a thick paste. Add the kumara, mussels, seasoning and herbs. Place spoonfuls of mixture into a hot oiled pan, cooking a couple of minutes on each side. Serve with a sweet chilli dipping sauce. **Makes 12.**

SMOKED TROUT OR SALMON MOUSSE

250g smoked trout or salmon
300ml sour cream
Juice of 1 lemon
1 tsp horseradish cream
2 tsp dill, chopped

Place all the ingredients in a food processor and blend until smooth. Season with salt and pepper.

WHITEBAIT FRITTERS WITH SWEET POTATO CHIPS

150g New Zealand whitebait
1 egg, beaten
Pinch of salt
Freshly ground black pepper
1 tbsp butter
2 kumara (New Zealand sweet potato),
    peeled
2 tbsp vegetable oil
A little plain flour, or rice flour
Lemon wedges and mayonnaise
    for serving

Cut the peeled kumara into wedges. Season and fry in a pan with a little butter and oil until golden. Finish cooking in a hot oven if necessary. Reserve some whitebait for frying whole. To make the fritters add just enough egg to combine the whitebait. Season and fry in a little oil and butter. Sprinkle the reserved whitebait with a little flour or rice flour. Place the whitebait in a sieve and shake off the excess flour. Fry in the oil and butter. Serve with lemon wedges, mayonnaise and the kumara chips.

SCALLOPS WITH BLACK GARLIC AND CHORIZO

250g small scallops, roe removed
50g chorizo sausage, finely chopped
5 cloves black garlic, peeled and
    finely sliced
Juice of half a lemon
1 tbsp parsley, finely chopped
1 tbsp chives, finely chopped
1 tbsp sherry
Lemon wedges to serve

Black Garlic
It is much easier to purchase black garlic but if wanting to make your own, wrap the garlic corms in foil. Find a 60C environment such as a plate warmer, oven, or dehydrator. Leave the garlic at that temperature (traditionally) for forty days. The garlic will become a deep, inky black colour and will be soft and sweet. If you have an Aga cooker place in the warming oven for several days.

Fry the diced chorizo. Remove from the pan and set aside. In the same pan sear the scallops on a high heat taking care not to cook too many at a time and not to overcook them. Remove from the pan and deglaze the pan with the lemon juice and sherry and add the parsley and chives. To assemble place a scallop in the base of a Chinese spoon, add some chorizo and a sliver or two of black garlic and drizzle with the pan juices.

Variation
Serve the scallop on pumpkin purée and garnish with chorizo.

MACADAMIA CRUSTED SCALLOPS

6 large scallops
100g macadamia nuts, chopped
Sea salt and pepper
1 small egg beaten
A little oil for frying

Sauce
Juice of 1 orange and some zest
2 tbsp Japanese plum vinegar

Mix the chopped macadamia nuts, salt and pepper together. Dip the scallops in the beaten egg then into the macadamia nut mixture. Fry in small batches in a hot pan taking care not to burn or overcook, or bake in a preheated 170C oven until slightly golden - just a few minutes. Serve with the sauce.

Mix the juice of the orange, the zest and the plum vinegar together.

Variation
Dip the scallops into a good dukkah mix.

SCALLOPS IN CIDER BATTER

75g plain four
1 egg, separated
1 tbsp olive oil
75ml cider, warm
300g scallops, cleaned
Vegetable oil for frying
Salt and pepper
Lemon wedges to serve

Mix the flour and salt in a bowl. Make a well in the centre and set aside. In a separate bowl whisk the egg yolk with the olive oil and cider together. Pour the liquid into the flour and stir until just combined. In another bowl whisk the egg white until stiff. Gently fold into the cider batter. Heat the oil to 190C. Season the scallops, dip into the batter and fry in small batches. Drain on kitchen paper and serve with lemon wedges.

SCALLOP AND SWEETCORN CAKES

¾ cup self raising flour
¼ cup polenta
2 egg yolks
1 tsp baking powder
¾ cup milk
¼ tsp Mexican chilli powder
Salt and freshly ground black pepper
200g corn kernels, drained
1 tbsp coriander, chopped
2 spring onions, finely chopped
3 large egg whites
10 scallops, white part only,
    cleaned and diced

Mix the flour, polenta, egg yolks, baking powder, milk, chilli powder, salt and pepper to form a fairly thick but dropping mixture. Add the corn, coriander and spring onions. Beat the egg whites until stiff and gently fold into the batter. Add the scallops and cook immediately in a heated, lightly oiled pan. Top with guacamole.

SCALLOPS WITH PERSIMMON AND FENNEL SALAD, LEMON INFUSED OIL

12 scallops
2 spring onions, julienned
2 small bulbs fennel, very finely sliced
1 tbsp lemon juice
2 tsp lemon infused oil plus extra
    for garnishing
1 non astringent persimmon (Fuji fruit)
6 mangetout, julienned
Baby salad leaves

Clean and trim the scallops and gently sear in a hot frying pan. Finely slice the persimmon and arrange several small slices in a Chinese spoon. Julienne a few slices and mix with the salad ingredients in a bowl. Combine a little lemon juice and lemon infused oil and dress the salad. Season. Arrange the salad and scallop in the spoons on top of the persimmon slices and drizzle with extra lemon infused oil if necessary.

POLENTA ROUNDS TOPPED WTH A QUENELLE OF SALT COD

500g boneless salt cod
450ml milk
3 sprigs parsley, 1 of thyme and
    1 bay leaf tied together
1 onion, quartered
1 large clove garlic
2-3 black peppercorns
375g floury potatoes, peeled and diced
2 tbsp walnut oil
1 clove garlic, crushed
2 hard boiled eggs, peeled and pressed
    through a sieve
1 tbsp parsley, finely chopped
Squeeze of lemon juice.
Capers to garnish

Soak the cod in water for 24 hours, changing the water several times and adding half the milk for the last soaking. Rinse the cod again. Cut the cod into several pieces and place in a saucepan with the herbs, onion, garlic clove and peppercorns. Cover with water and bring to the boil gently. Simmer for a couple of minutes only then remove from the heat and allow to rest in the liquid for about 15 minutes. Remove the fish using a slotted spoon and set aside. Boil the potatoes in the poaching liquid and when cooked mash. Whisk in a little of the walnut oil and the crushed garlic. Remove the skin from the fish and debone. In a food processor pulse with a little warm milk and walnut oil. Mix into the mashed potatoes and add the sieved hard boiled egg and the parsley. Season and add a little lemon juice. Serve on polenta rounds with tomato sauce and garnish with parsley and capers.

Polenta rounds
500ml vegetable or light fish stock
500ml milk
170g polenta
30g butter

Bring the stock and the milk to the boil in a large saucepan. Whisk in the polenta. Reduce the heat to low and continue to cook for a further 3-5 minutes whisking constantly. Stir in the butter. Grease a 26 x 16cm tin. Pour in the polenta mixture and set aside for several hours to cool and set. Turn out on a board and using a 4.5 cm pastry cutter cut the polenta into 24 rounds. Gently fry when ready to serve and top with tomato sauce, a quenelle of salt cod and a caper.

Tomato sauce
8 large ripe tomatoes
1 small shallot
1 clove garlic
2 tbsp olive oil
1 tbsp tomato paste
Salt and freshly ground black pepper

Peel the tomatoes by blanching in hot water. Gently sauté the shallot and the garlic, add the tomato and cook gently until well cooked. Towards the end of cooking add the tomato paste and salt and pepper. Purée and sieve before use.

SALT COD CROQUETTES

Salt cod mixture (as in previous recipe)
2 eggs
A little plain flour
2 tbsp milk
Panko or regular breadcrumbs
Vegetable oil for frying

Mix 1 of the eggs into the salt cod mixture. Shape into croquettes. Mix the milk and the other egg together. Dip the croquettes into the flour, then into the egg wash, then the panko crumbs. Deep fry in small batches. Serve with the tomato sauce as in previous recipe.

POTTED SHRIMP

1 kg prawns, cooked, peeled and deveined
½ tsp lemon zest
¼ tsp freshly grated nutmeg
¼ tsp cayenne pepper
¼ tsp allspice
300g unsalted butter
2 tbsp parsley, finely chopped

In a food processor pulse the prawns and the spices. Heat the butter over low heat. Allow the butter to rest. Skim the foam from the top and pour the remaining butter into a jug leaving the solids behind. Add half the butter and parsley to the prawns. Divide the mixture into individual ramekin dishes. Pour over the remaining butter and refrigerate until set. Serve with Melba toast.

ARBROATH SMOKIE PATĒ

200g Arbroath smokies, skinned and
    deboned
2 tsp of gelatine
100ml fish stock
100ml double cream
1 tsp sherry or juice of ½ lemon
Salt and pepper

Heat the fish stock and dissolve the gelatine. Cool. Process the smokies in a food processor adding the dissolved gelatine and sherry or lemon juice until smooth. Season. Gently work in the cream. Set in a parchment lined loaf tin. To serve: make quenelles with a hot, wet spoon. Serve with Melba toast.

SMOKED SALMON ON PURPLE POTATOES, WHITE BEADS AND CAVIAR

12 small purple potatoes
Olive oil
75-100g smoked salmon, chopped
    very fine
1 tbsp red onion or shallot finely
    chopped
1 tsp crème fraîche
Zest of ½ lemon
1 tsp chives, chopped
Dill to garnish
Salt and pepper
Ikura, or any other type of caviar
    to garnish

Clean the potatoes and boil in salted water with the skin on. Gently simmer for about 7-8 minutes or until just cooked. Do not overcook. Drain and cool. Then peel. Combine the smoked salmon, red onion, crème fraîche, lemon zest and chives. Season and mix well. Trim the ends from the potatoes and slice into 2cm slices. With a melon baller, make an indentation in the potato. Brush with olive oil. Season lightly with salt and pepper. Fill the potatoes with the salmon mixture and garnish with ikura or caviar and a few egg white pearls and chives. Refrigerate until ready to serve.

Egg white pearls
500 ml grapeseed oil
50 ml egg white, strained

Heat the grapeseed oil in a small pan to 70C only. Using an eye dropper drop the strained egg white drop by drop into the oil in rapid succession. Remove the pearls from the oil using a fine sieve.

SCALLOP, HONEYDEW AND CORIANDER SALAD WITH GINGER DRESSING

6 trimmed and cleaned scallops
1 small carrot julienned
3 mangetout, blanched and julienned
100g honeydew melon, julienned
1 tbsp fresh coriander, finely chopped
1 tsp chopped chives
Flesh from 1 finger lime

Firstly make the dressing. To make ginger juice, finely grate the fresh ginger and squeeze to obtain the juice. Mix with the other ingredients and set aside. For the salad, mix the julienned carrot, melon, mangetout, chives and coriander. Add half the dressing. Sear the scallops. To serve, arrange the salad on a small dish, top with the seared scallop and garnish with lime beads. Drizzle with the extra dressing.

Ginger dressing
2 tsp lemon juice
1 tsp ginger juice
1 tsp fish sauce
2-3 tsp caster sugar
1 tbsp vegetable oil

Mix all the ingredients together.

POTTED SMOKED TROUT

1 smoked trout, skinned and deboned
½ small lemon, zest and juice
2 tbsp sour cream
1 tsp aniseed, finely chopped
2 spring onion, finely chopped
2 tsp fresh dill, finely chopped
Salt and fresh black pepper
Spring onions, green part only to garnish
Dill to garnish
Blinis, Melba toast or lavosh for serving
Lemon wedges to serve

Flake the trout fillet into even pieces. Add the sour cream, lemon zest and juice, chopped aniseed and spring onion and dill. Mix well and season with salt and pepper. Line a ramekin with the green part of a large spring onion which has been softened by dipping into hot water. Fill with the smoked trout mixture and garnish with dill and lemon. Serve with blinis, Melba toast or lavosh.

MELBA TOAST

Slices of white bread

Toast the slices of bread, only a couple slices at a time, and while still warm remove the crusts and with a sharp knife slice the bread between the two toasted sides. Cut each slice on the diagonal. Brown under a hot grill taking care not to burn.

SALMON AND RICE FLOUR PATTIES

80g ground rice
2 cloves garlic, crushed
3-4 red chillies, finely chopped
2 stems lemongrass, finely chopped
100g spring onion, finely chopped
300ml coconut milk
2 tbsp fish sauce
2 tsp palm sugar
8 stems dill, chopped
8 kaffir lime leaves, finely chopped
150g salmon fillet, finely chopped
Avocado to garnish, optional
Sweet chilli sauce

In a blender process the garlic, chillies, lemongrass and spring onion with the coconut milk, fish sauce and sugar. Add the ground rice and mix. Allow the mixture to rest for at least an hour. Add the dill and kaffir lime leaves and finely chopped salmon fillet. Cook as you would a blini. Garnish with avocado and sweet chilli sauce.

POTATO TOPPED SALMON PATTIES

225g salmon fillet including a little
    smoked salmon, chopped into
    small pieces
2 spring onions, finely chopped
3 tbsp red pepper, finely chopped
1 egg
2 tbsp sour cream
2 tbsp lemon juice
2 tbsp flat leaf parsley, finely chopped
2 cloves garlic, crushed
1 hot chilli
½ tsp salt

Creamy mashed potatoes with butter
Dill to garnish

Process all the ingredients in a food processor without overworking. Line muffin tins with patty cases and place a spoonful of the mixture into each. Top with mashed potato and cook in a moderate oven until the salmon is just cooked and the potato is beginning to turn golden. Serve warm.

CRAB BEIGNETS

60g butter
300ml water
½ cup plain flour
2 eggs
200g crab meat
¼ cup chopped mushrooms
1 tsp ground ginger
1 tbsp mayonnaise
1 tbsp slivered almonds, toasted
2 tsp chopped chives
1½ cups vegetable oil

Bring to a simmer the water and the butter. Remove from the heat and add the flour. Return to the heat and beat constantly with a wooden spoon until the mixture forms a smooth paste which leaves the sides of the pan. Cool slightly. Add the eggs one at a time beating well after each addition. Stir in the crab, mushrooms, ginger, mayonnaise, almonds and chives. Heat the oil and fry spoonfuls at a time. Serve with teriyaki dipping sauce.

Teriyaki dipping sauce
½ cup teriyaki sauce
2 tbsp vinegar
1 tsp sesame oil

Mix all the ingredients together.

TEMPURA BATTER FOR PRAWNS, SCALLOPS, CALAMARI, FISH GOUJONS AND VEGETABLES

Commercially available tempura mixes are excellent, but this recipe is also very easy to prepare.

1 egg
1 cup icy cold water or crushed ice
¾ cup plain flour
Pinch of bicarbonate of soda

Beat the egg and the water together until light and fluffy. Add the flour and bicarbonate of soda to the egg mixture and mix together quickly. Do not over beat. The batter should be very thin. Add more iced water if necessary. Use immediately and fry in very hot vegetable oil and serve with one of the dipping sauces.

SALT AND PEPPER SPICE MIX FOR PRAWNS, SCALLOPS, CALAMARI OR FISH GOUJONS

1 tbsp Sichuan pepper
1 tsp black pepper
2 tsp flaked sea salt
2 tbsp rice flour

Dry roast the Sichuan pepper and black peppercorns in a small frying pan over low heat then cool. Grind them and combine with the salt and rice flour. Toss the seafood to coat and deep fry for a couple of minutes. Drain and serve with a dipping sauce.

DIPPING SAUCES

Coriander, lemon and sesame

1 cup lemon juice
½ cup water
1 cup palm sugar
½ bunch coriander - leaves and
    root, finely chopped
2 tbsp sesame seeds
Salt to taste

Make a syrup by bringing the
water to the boil and add the
palm sugar. Add the other
ingredients when cool.

Lime, ginger and soy

¼ cup fresh lime juice
15ml rice vinegar
1 tsp fresh ginger, grated
1 tsp wasabi paste
30ml Japanese soy sauce, tamari
15ml mirin
1 tsp sesame oil
1 tbsp brown sugar
100ml grapeseed or rice bran oil

Mix all the ingredients except the
oil in a blender. With the blade
running add the oil in a slow
steady stream.

Lime and chilli

70g palm sugar
1 clove garlic
1 tbsp coriander leaves,
    finely chopped
1 tbsp rice vinegar
1 small chilli
⅓ cup lime juice

Dissolve palm sugar and rice
vinegar over a little heat. Cool
then add the garlic, chilli and
coriander. Whisk in the lime
juice and season to taste with
sea salt and black pepper.

Mango, chilli and lime mayonnaise

1 ripe mango, peeled
1 small red chilli, finely
    chopped
1 lime, juice and zest
1 cup good mayonnaise
Salt and pepper

Remove the mango flesh from
the stone and place in a blender.
Add the chilli, juice and zest of
the lime and the mayonnaise.
Blend until smooth. Season
to taste.

Mirin for oysters

1 tsp fresh ginger, grated
4 tbsp rice wine vinegar
1 tsp sugar
1 tsp soy
6 tbsp grapeseed oil
2 tbsp mild olive oil
½ tbsp lemon juice

Mix all the ingredients
together.

Sweet chilli and ginger

100ml sweet chilli sauce
8 cloves garlic, crushed
1 ginger root
½ bunch coriander
1 tbsp sambal oelek
60ml lime juice
60ml soy
60ml sesame oil
15ml fish sauce
15ml rice vinegar

Mix all the ingredients
together.

Spiced oil

1 ½ tbsp soy
1 ½ tbsp white vinegar
2 ½ tbsp balsamic vinegar
100ml light olive oil
½ tsp sambal oelek
1 tbsp lime juice

Mix all the ingredients
together.

SALMON WITH KECAP MANIS MARINADE

Salmon fillet, skinned and deboned
Nori sheets
Bamboo sticks to serve

Cut the salmon fillet into 2.5cm strips across the fillet. Marinate the salmon in the marinade for an hour or two. Wrap each fillet in nori then cut into equal serving portions. Place a bamboo skewer in the end of each piece. Place on a parchment lined baking tray and cook in a 150C oven until just cooked.

Marinade

Equal amounts of kecap manis and
    rice wine vinegar
Chilli to taste
Squeeze of lemon or lime juice
Fresh coriander leaves, finely chopped

Mix all the ingredients together.

Variation

Cut the salmon into longer strips and wrap with squid ink linguini.

SALMON FILLET WITH SUMAC AND LIME

250g salmon fillet
Zest of 1 lime
½ tsp chilli powder or cayenne pepper
1 tsp sumac
Salt
2 tbsp good mayonnaise
A dash of Sambuca

Firstly skin the salmon fillet and cut into about six 2cm x 2 cm x 6cm portions. Dry the lime zest in a low oven for about 30 minutes. Mix the spices and dried lime zest and coat the salmon pieces. Put each piece of salmon onto a serving skewer. Sear the salmon in a hot pan or barbecue and cook until just cooked. Serve with slices of lime or mayonnaise with a dash of Sambuca added.

CARDAMOM AND CORIANDER FISH

2 bunches coriander, including roots
Zest and juice of 1 lime
2 cloves garlic, crushed
1 tsp cardamom seeds, crushed
1 tsp fresh ginger, grated
2 tbsp vegetable oil
Salt and freshly ground black pepper
500g firm white fish fillets cut into
    2.5 cm strips
1 cup plain yoghurt

Pulse the first 7 ingredients to a smooth paste. Using only half of the mixture coat the fish strips and marinate for several hours. Thread onto skewers and spray with oil. Pan fry or barbecue. Mix the remainder of the marinade with the yoghurt and serve with the fish.

COCONUT FRIED FISH

400g firm white fish cut into 2.5cm dice
1 cup rice flour
Salt and pepper
1 egg, beaten
60-100g desiccated coconut
Vegetable oil for frying

Season the rice flour. Toss the fish in the flour, dip into the egg then roll in the coconut. Fry in small batches in oil heated to 190C.

Variation

Season the rice flour with 1 tbsp furikake (Japanese seasoning) which includes sesame seed and seaweed. Omit the coconut. Serve with a dipping sauce. Coat the fish with a good quality dukkah.

POTATO CRISPS WITH PRAWNS

200g sweet potato, peeled
100g small prawns, peeled
1 egg white
2 cloves garlic, crushed
2 tbsp cornflour
1 tbsp cold water
½ tsp white pepper
Vegetable oil for frying

Finely julienne the sweet potato and place in a bowl with the garlic, prawns and egg white. Mix the cornflour with the cold water and add to the sweet potato and prawn mix. (If serving with the nori wrapped prawns and tempura shiso leaves use a little of the tempura batter to bind the potato and prawns). Season. Heat the oil to 175C. Fry in small batches making sure to drain excess liquid before doing so. Best cooked just before serving.

Variation

Wrap each prawn with cooked rice noodles, or vegetable or squid ink spaghetti, and add seaweed seasoning or coriander to the batter mix.

COCONUT AND CORIANDER FISH CAKES

1 cup (150g) self raising flour
2 eggs
Salt and freshly ground black pepper
½ cup water
300g fresh fish, boned and
    diced into 1-2cm dices
½ cup desiccated coconut,
    lightly toasted
1 ripe banana, peeled and mashed
¼ cup fresh coriander leaf, chopped
2 tbsp sweet chilli sauce
Vegetable oil for frying

Mix the flour, eggs and salt and pepper with the water to make a batter. Mix in all the other ingredients, except the oil. Allow to stand in the refrigerator for at least 1 hour before cooking. Fry in small batches in a medium to hot frying pan. Serve with fresh mango salsa.

Mango salsa
1 mango, finely diced
1 tbsp sweet chilli sauce
1 tbsp fresh lime juice
1 tbsp fresh coriander, finely chopped

Mix all the ingredients together.

THAI FISH CAKES

1 kg fresh cod fillet or any fresh
    firm white fish
⅓ cup red curry paste
2 tbsp chopped fresh coriander
2 tsp sugar
100g thinly sliced fine beans
1 tbsp fish sauce

Finely chop the fish with the red curry paste. Process in a food processor until smooth. Add the other ingredients and season to taste. Roll into small balls, flatten and shallow fry until just cooked. Serve with sweet chilli dipping sauce or cucumber sauce.

Cucumber sauce
1 small cucumber, peeled and
    finely chopped
⅓ tbsp sugar
½ cup rice vinegar
2 tbsp hot water
1 tsp salt
1-2 red chillies, finely chopped
3 spring onions, finely chopped
Coriander to garnish

Dissolve the sugar and salt in the vinegar. Add the cucumber, chilli and spring onions. Garnish with coriander.

NORI WRAPPED PRAWNS WITH TEMPURA SHISO LEAVES AND SALMON ROE

Large cooked prawns, peeled
    leaving tails attached
A couple of sheets of nori, cut into
    2cm strips
Togarashi - nanami or schichimi
    (Japanese pepper flakes), optional
4 tbsp mayonnaise
1 tsp mango chutney
1 lime, zest and juice
1 tsp sweet chilli sauce
Shiso leaves or curly kale
Tempura batter
Vegetable oil for frying
Salmon roe (ikura)

Wrap each prawn with a strip of nori, dampening the end so it will stick to itself. For the sauce blend together the mayonnaise, mango chutney, lime zest and sweet chilli sauce. Add lime juice to achieve the desired taste. Place a couple of spoonfuls of the mayonnaise into the base of cocktail glasses. Top with a prawn and sprinkle with the togarashi if using. For the tempura shiso prepare the tempura batter. Heat the oil to 180C. Dip each leaf into the batter and fry in the hot oil until the batter has puffed up - only about 30 seconds. Do not try to cook too many at once. Top with salmon roe.

CRISP BETEL LEAVES, CURLY KALE OR SHISO

2 tbsp red curry paste
100g rice flour
2 tsp ground turmeric
1 tbsp fish sauce
3 kaffir lime leaves, finely sliced
Vegetable oil for deep frying
18 betel leaves
200g small raw prawns, shelled and
    halved
2 tbsp roasted peanuts, diced
Sweet chilli sauce to serve

Combine the curry paste, rice flour and turmeric in a bowl. Add fish sauce and 50ml cold water and mix well. Heat vegetable oil in a wok over medium high heat. Dip the betel leaves in the red curry mixture. Place a few in the hot oil and carefully put half a prawn on top of each. Cook leaves and prawns until golden and crisp. Drain on paper towel. Serve sprinkled with roasted peanuts and accompanied by sweet chilli sauce. **Serves 6.**

SARDINE AND SPINACH PATÈ

340g frozen chopped spinach
130g sardines, drained
50g anchovy fillets, drained
50g butter, melted

Defrost the spinach and squeeze out as much liquid as possible. Sweat in the butter. Cool slightly and put in a food processor with the other ingredients. Process until smooth. Put into a serving dish and chill at least a couple of hours before serving.

RILLETTES OF SMOKED EEL AND SMOKED TROUT

450g fresh smoked eel
1 fresh smoked trout
Salt and freshly ground black pepper
Cayenne pepper
150ml double cream
Lemon juice

Skin the eel, and the trout. Debone both. Purée a third of the eel and all of the trout in a food processor. Season. Add half of the cream and the juice of ¼ lemon and process until smooth. Add the remaining cream and season with more lemon juice, salt and pepper. Process until well mixed. Transfer the mixture to a bowl. Cut the remaining eel into thin strips and gently fold into the eel and trout mixture. When ready to serve shape into quenelles using two spoons and serve with croutons.

VICHYSSOISE MOUSSE WITH BLANCHED LEEKS AND SMOKED OYSTER

50g butter
100g leek, finely sliced,
2 shallots, finely diced
1 clove garlic, crushed
500ml chicken stock
100g mashing potatoes, peeled and diced
125ml cream
Salt and pepper
2 tsp gelatine
Sliced white sandwich bread
1 tin smoked oysters
1 leek, white part only sliced
    finely into 7cm strips
A knob of butter

Sweat the leek, shallots and garlic in the butter. Add the potato and cook for another couple of minutes without browning. Add the stock and simmer until all the vegetables are well cooked. Remove from the heat and cool a little. Transfer to a blender and process until smooth. Add the cream and blend only to mix. Season. Strain into a bowl. Mix the gelatine with a little warm water to dissolve. Mix well into the Vichyssoise mixture. Pour into a 2 cm deep tray and allow to set. Cut 4 cm rounds from the sliced bread and lightly dry out in a low oven. When ready to assemble cut 4 cm rounds from the set Vichyssoise and place between two toast rounds. Sweat the leek strips in the butter. Place an oyster on top of the toast. Garnish with the leek and drizzle with the oil from the oysters.

SEAWEED WAFER CUPS WITH SCALLOPS AND MISO FLAN

Scallops
Hoisin sauce
Micro herbs for garnishing
Caviar for garnishing

Sear the scallops in a hot pan. Brush with hoisin and flash again in the pan. To assemble. Place some miso custard in the base of the seaweed wafers just before serving. Top with a scallop and garnish with micro herbs and caviar.

Miso custard
20g white miso paste
40g dashi - or 1 tsp of furikake seasoning
    instead of the miso and dashi
60g cream
1 whole egg
2 egg yolks

Mix all the ingredients together. Cook in a bain-marie in a 180C oven until set. Allow to cool before portioning into the shaped wafers just before serving.

Seaweed wafer cups
4g wakame seaweed
80g plain flour
100g butter, melted
100g egg whites (about 3 eggs)
20g icing sugar
Salt and pepper

In a blender pulse the wakame to little more than a powder. Add the other ingredients and mix well. Line a baking tray with parchment paper. Put a small spoonful of the mixture onto the parchment paper. The mixture will spread during cooking. Place a piece of parchment paper on top of the wafer and using your fingers gently spread the wafer into the right shape and thinner. It is easier to leave the parchment paper on top of the wafer and remove during cooking. Bake at 160C until golden. Shape over a dariole mould immediately after removing from the oven. Store in an airtight container. **Makes 35.**

TUNA WITH SPICES

Tuna fillet, cut into 2.5cm pieces
2 tbsp light soy
2 tbsp mirin
1 tbsp sesame oil
½ tsp five spice
1 tsp sugar
1 tsp salt
1 tsp Sichuan pepper
1 tsp cumin
Oil for frying

Mix the soy, mirin and sesame oil and marinate the tuna for an hour or two. Drain. Mix the spices together and dust the tuna pieces in the mixture. Gently pan fry.

"I've tried but it's always in vain, not to drink so much champagne. But when I'm in trouble I do need that bubble and it happens again and again."

Rupert Brooke

6

DIPS, EGGS & SOUP SHOTS

Guests like to be quickly comfortable and presented with the most simplest of offerings representing goodwill, warmth and ease. It may seem old fashioned, but a bowl of olives or a series of dips will always settle the arriving throng. The dip recipes fill me with memories of idle days in some taverna on a Greek Island, or sipping a tipple of tequilla in a Mexican bar.

Nibbles that are completely self-contained are a gem, as one can have them lined up and ready to go in a flash. Soups, as with pastry, are popular and offer that little palate surprise and touch of comfort. A collection of small shot glasses and cups are a wise purchase and are a great addition to the catering cupboard. They can be washed and recycled and always look stylish when served; they can also be juggled easily when guests are standing.

Eggs, too, are always a hit. Quail eggs and petite egg sandwiches are often served at my Highland parties.

Just keep it simple and you can't go wrong.

GUACAMOLE

3 medium ripe avocados
½ green pepper
3 tsp lemon juice
1 ½ red chillies, seeds removed
2 tsp olive oil
2 spring onions
½ tsp ground coriander
1 ripe medium tomato, skinned
1 hard boiled egg
Small bunch fresh coriander
Salt and pepper

Finely chop all the ingredients and mix together. Add more lemon juice if necessary. Season and serve with fresh tortilla or corn chips.

SMOKED TOMATO DIP

2 shallots, diced
Splash liquid smoke flavour*
2 cloves garlic
170ml sherry
150g cherry tomatoes
1 tbsp sugar
2 tsp fresh oregano
1 tsp black pepper
1 tsp salt
Mascarpone
Breadcrumbs
* Available in delis

Skin the tomatoes by blanching in boiling water. Place in a bowl and add a splash of liquid smoke, salt and freshly ground black pepper. Slow roast in a low oven for a couple of hours. Sauté the shallots and garlic. In a food processor purée the tomato, shallots, and garlic. Add mascarpone and enough breadcrumbs to bring to the desired consistency. Add a pinch of sugar to taste if desired.

CHICKPEA AND PUMPKIN DIP

400g tin chickpeas, drained and rinsed
800g pumpkin, diced
Olive oil
1 tsp sweet paprika
Pinch of dried chilli flakes
¼ cup lemon juice

Toss the pumpkin in enough olive oil to coat, season to taste with salt and cracked black pepper, and roast. Blend with the chickpeas and add lemon juice and chilli flakes to taste. Serve warm with pita bread or lavosh.

NACHOS SAUCE

1 ½ medium onions, finely chopped
3 cloves garlic, peeled and crushed
¼ cup olive oil
¼ cup plain flour
½ tsp cumin
½ tsp ground coriander
¼ tsp cayenne pepper
1 red pepper, finely diced
2 medium tomatoes, chopped
1 tsp salt
¼ tsp black pepper
345ml beer
2 tsp sugar
2 cups mild grated cheese

Simmer all the ingredients (except cheese) for an hour or so, mixing the flour with the liquid to avoid lumps. Then add the cheddar. Serve with corn chips.

ASPARAGUS SPEARS WITH DULCE DE LECHE AND WASABI SAUCE

Thick asparagus spears
Sea salt for garnish
Extra-virgin olive oil
Flowers to garnish, optional

Trim the asparagus and blanch. Refresh in iced water. Arrange on a serving platter and drizzle with olive oil and sprinkle with the sea salt. Garnish with flowers. Serve with a small dish of dulce de leche and wasabi dipping sauce.

Dulce de leche
2 litres goats milk
¼ cup dark-brown sugar
Pinch of salt

Gently simmer the goats milk, brown sugar and salt over low heat in a heavy bottomed saucepan. Allow to reduce for about 3 hours until 1 cup remains.

Sauce
Dulce de leche
Wasabi paste
Salt

Mix dulce de leche with a little wasabi paste. Season and mix well. Present in a small dipping bowl.

WATERMELON WITH BALSAMIC, BASIL LEAF AND PARMESAN

Watermelon cut into 4 x 2 x 2cm
    rectangles
Balsamic dressing
Basil leaves
Parmesan

Using a melon baller make an indentation in the top of the watermelon rectangle. Add a little balsamic dressing, a basil leaf and a shaving of Parmesan.

BLOODY MARY OYSTER SHOTS

250ml vodka
375ml tomato juice, or Clamato
1 dash of Worcestershire sauce, to taste
1 dash of Tabasco, to taste
1 pinch celery salt, to taste
1 dash of lemon juice, to taste
10 fresh oysters
Horseradish (optional)
Celery stalk, cut into strands, to garnish.

Mix the vodka and tomato juice (or Clamato) and add the Worcestershire sauce, Tabasco, celery salt and lemon juice to taste. Put an oyster in the bottom of each of 10 shot glasses and pour over the Bloody Mary mix. Garnish with a few celery strands before serving. **Makes 10 shots.**

JAPANESE INSPIRED OYSTER SHOTS

10 fresh oysters
½ teaspoon wasabi paste, optional
½ teaspoon pickled ginger, shredded,
    optional
500ml mirin
125ml sake
40ml rice wine vinegar
25ml light soy
1 tbsp wasabi powder

In a large stainless steel saucepan combine the mirin and sake. Bring to a gentle simmer. Flambé the sake mix carefully until the alcohol has been burnt off. Cool. Add the vinegar. Taste for a balance of sweet and sour and adjust if necessary. Add soy for colour and flavour before stirring in the wasabi powder. Refrigerate until the wasabi powder has fallen to the bottom of the container and a clear liquid is left. Strain off the liquid into another jug making sure not to disturb the impurities at the bottom. Store in the refrigerator until ready to use. Place an oyster in the bottom of a shot glass. Top with the shooter mix. The oyster should float. Top with a little pickled ginger and wasabi paste. Serve chilled.

QUAIL EGG SCOTCH EGGS

1 dozen quail eggs
300g chicken and rocket, or chicken and
    chive sausage meat
500ml of vegetable oil for deep frying

Soft boil the eggs then peel. Wrap each egg with the chicken mixture. Fry in small batches in the oil. Serve with the curry mayonnaise.

Variation
Pulse 175g of smoked trout or salmon fillet with just enough double cream to bring the mixture together. Season and add herbs of choice. Wrap the eggs with the mixture, dip in beaten egg, then crumbs, and deep fry.

Curry mayonnaise
1 dsp olive oil
½ spring onion, finely diced
1 tbsp curry powder
Juice of ½ lime, or ¼ lemon
2 tbsp crème fraîche
150ml mayonnaise
1 tbsp mango chutney

Mix all the ingredients together.

> **Note:** To soft boil quail eggs place into a saucepan of boiling water. Bring back to the boil. For a soft yolk cook for only two minutes from the point of a fast simmer. Drain the eggs immediately and plunge into iced water to halt the cooking process and cool completely. Do not cook too many in the same pot.

TEA SMOKED QUAIL EGGS

12 quail eggs - larger sized ones
2 tbsp coarse salt
4 tbsp dark soy sauce
2 whole star anise or 1 tsp aniseed
2 tbsp smoky tea such as
    Lapsang Souchong

Boil the eggs for 4 minutes over a gentle heat. Drain. Then tap the shells all over until the shell is completely cracked. Do not peel. Return the eggs to a saucepan, cover with cold water and add the salt, soy, star anise and tea. Bring to a boil, reduce the heat and simmer very slowly for about 2 hours. Leave the eggs in the liquid for about 8 hours. Peel then serve.

SMOKED SALMON AND WATERCRESS PINWHEELS

4 slices brown bread
50g cream cheese
100g smoked salmon
Small bunch watercress leaves

Trim the crusts from the bread and roll thin using a rolling pin. Spread with cream cheese, then a layer of watercress, then smoked salmon. Roll the bread up tightly. Leave in the refrigerator for a couple of hours before slicing into bite-size pinwheels.

EGG AND CAVIAR SANDWICHES

Slices of white sandwich bread
Butter, softened for spreading
Eggs, hard boiled
Mayonnaise
Chives
Salt and pepper
Lumpfish caviar

Grate the boiled eggs, add the chives and enough mayonnaise to hold the eggs together. Season. Butter the slices of white bread. Using a 4 cm canape cutter, cut rounds from the buttered bread. Use the same cutter for assembly of the sandwiches. Place a bread round on the base, top with the egg mayonnaise and then add a layer of lumpfish caviar. Finish with a buttered bread round.

SWEET POTATO BALLS WITH COCONUT

125ml vegetable oil
1.2 kg sweet potatoes, peeled
Salt
225g plain flour
5 dried chillies
8 shallots, peeled
½ tsp turmeric
2.5cm ginger, finely chopped
3 stalks lemongrass, finely chopped
3 tbsp dried prawns, soaked in
    cold water and drained
1 tsp ground coriander
½ tsp ground fennel seeds
½ tsp ground cumin seeds
200g grated coconut
500ml water
1 tsp salt
Oil for frying

Boil the sweet potatoes in salted water until tender. Mash and add the flour and knead to form a soft dough. Set aside and prepare the prawn and chilli paste by processing together the chillies, shallots, turmeric, ginger, lemongrass and dried prawns. Heat the oil in the pan and fry the finely ground paste until fragrant. Add the grated coconut and water and stir well. Add the coriander, fennel and cumin. Bring to the boil and cook until the mixture becomes dry, stirring all the time. Remove from the heat and allow to cool. To assemble divide the dough into 40 portions. Roll and flatten each ball and place 2 tsp of the coconut mixture in the centre. Wrap the edges of the dough over the filling and roll into a ball. Place on a floured tray. Deep fry the balls in the oil.

SWEET POTATO AND BACON BALLS

400g bacon, finely diced
800g sweet potato, grated
Pinch sugar
¼ tsp nutmeg
Salt and pepper
2 eggs
2 tbsp cornflour

Mix together and roll into balls and deep fry.

CHILLED LEMONGRASS AND CORIANDER VICHYSSOISE

2 medium onions
60g butter
4 thick stems lemongrass
4 spring onions
60g coriander leaves
300g new potatoes
1 litre chicken stock with lemongrass and
    coriander trimmings added
150ml milk
Salt and pepper

Sweat the onions in the butter. Add the other ingredients and gently simmer until cooked. Allow to cool slightly before blending. Strain through a fine sieve before serving.

COCONUT AND LEMONGRASS SOUP

2 tbsp olive oil
50g butter
3 shallots, finely chopped
2.5cm fresh ginger, finely chopped
1 tsp cumin
2 tsp curry powder
3 tbsp dried coconut
2 curry leaves
2 stalks lemongrass
500ml coconut milk
500ml cream
800ml chicken stock
2 tbsp fresh coriander, finely chopped,
    to garnish

Sweat the shallots in a little olive oil and butter, gradually add the ginger, cumin, curry powder, dried coconut, curry leaves and lemongrass. Add the coconut milk and cream and simmer to reduce slightly. In a separate saucepan heat the stock and add to the coconut mixture and bring to the desired consistency. Season and cook for about 20 minutes. Strain through a fine sieve and reheat to serve. Garnish with the coriander.

FENNEL AND ALMOND SOUP

200g fennel bulb, finely diced
1 medium green pepper, finely diced
1 small onion, finely diced
½ tbsp caster sugar
75g ground almonds
1 litre vegetable or chicken stock
Salt and pepper
Sprigs of dill to garnish

Place the ingredients, except the almonds and dill, in a saucepan and gently simmer until the vegetables are cooked. Add the almonds and season. Blend. Strain before serving. Garnish with dill.

CARROT SOUP WITH ANISE FOAM

800g carrots, peeled and
    roughly chopped
2 medium onions, diced
2 cloves garlic, crushed
3-4 tbsp butter
4 cups chicken stock
Dill stalks
1 ½ teaspoon salt
Whipping cream or milk
Shot of Sambuca

Sweat the onions, garlic and carrots in the butter without browning. Add the stock and dill and cook until the carrots are soft. Cool. Pureé the mixture in a blender. Strain through a sieve and season to taste. When ready to serve gently reheat. Pour into shot glasses and top with the anise foam. If in possession of a milk frother use milk for the topping and add Sambuca before foaming. Otherwise whip cream and add a shot of Sambuca.

GAZPACHO

2 cloves garlic
1 tsp salt
1 red pepper, cored and diced
1 large cucumber, peeled and diced
3 tbsp olive oil
1 green pepper, cored and diced
3 tbsp wine vinegar
1 small red onion, diced
400ml tomato juice
5 large tomatoes
4 slices stale white bread, crusts removed
1 tsp paprika
Several sprigs of parsley

Skin the tomatoes by plunging into boiling water and then into iced water. Blend with the other ingredients but reserve a little diced cucumber and parsley for garnish. Season. Cover and refrigerate for at least 4 hours before serving.

JERUSALEM ARTICHOKE SOUP

50g butter
2 tbsp olive oil
2 medium onions, chopped
750g artichokes, peeled
1.2 litres chicken or vegetable stock
Salt and pepper
2 tbsp chopped parsley
200ml cream
Croutons to garnish

Melt the butter, add the oil and fry the onion until soft without colouring. Add the stock and artichokes, cover and simmer until the artichokes are completely soft. Season and liquidise. Reheat with the cream and parsley. Serve with the croutons.

ZUCCHINI SOUP

1 kg zucchini, diced
1 medium onion, finely sliced
2 garlic cloves, crushed
2 tbsp butter
500ml chicken stock
125ml cream

Sauté the onion and garlic in the butter. Add the zucchini and sauté without browning. Add the stock and simmer until the zucchini is cooked. Season then cool slightly. Pureé and strain. Return to a saucepan, add the cream and simmer for a couple of minutes.

ROASTED RED PEPPER SOUP

6 red peppers
2 tomatoes
2 cloves garlic
1 litre chicken stock
1 sprig fresh oregano
Cream
Black pepper

Grill the peppers and tomatoes. Simmer with the garlic, stock and oregano. Season. Cool, add a little cream and blend and sieve. If wanting to serve the two soups together make sure they have the same consistency. Transfer the soups to jugs and with a jug in each hand slowly pour simultaneously. Serve with a few drops of parsley oil.

Parsley oil
1 bunch flat leaf parsley
80ml light olive oil
50ml grapeseed oil
Sea salt and pepper

Wash the parsley and finely chop the leaves. Process in a blender with the oil and seasoning. Strain through muslin overnight.

WILD MUSHROOM SOUP

Olive oil
500g wild mushrooms, trimmed and
    chopped
2 onions, finely chopped
3 cloves garlic, chopped
300ml white wine
750ml good chicken or vegetable stock
Salt and pepper
Parsley stalks
Cream, optional

Sauté the mushrooms in batches, then the onions and the garlic. Add the wine and cook to a syrupy consistency. Before adding the stock remove some of the mushroom mix to purée and use as a garnish. Add the stock and parsley stalks to the remaining mushroom and onion mix and simmer for about 30 minutes. Add cream if wishing to make a creamy soup. Allow to cool a little before seasoning and blending. Serve with a quenelle of mushroom purée.

CREAM PUMPKIN SOUP WITH PROSCIUTTO CRISPS

2 tbsp butter
1 onion, finely chopped
1 leek, white part only, finely sliced
1 garlic clove, crushed
1kg butternut pumpkin, peeled and diced
1 large fluffy potato, peeled and diced
½ tsp ground coriander
1 tsp ground cumin
½ tsp freshly grated nutmeg
1 litre chicken or vegetable stock
125ml pouring cream
Very thin prosciutto rashers to garnish

Sweat the onion, leek, garlic and butternut pumpkin in the butter without colouring. Add the spices, stock and potato and simmer until the pumpkin is tender and well cooked. Cool. In a blender purée the mixture then strain through a fine sieve. Add a dash of cream reserving the rest to garnish the soup. When ready to serve gently heat and add a swirl of cream. Garnish with a prosciutto crisp. To make the prosciutto crisps cut the rashers into long strips and twist around the handle of a wooden spoon. Place in a very low oven for a couple of hours to crisp.

SWEET POTATO AND COCONUT SOUP

1 kg sweet potato, peeled and diced
2 tsp vegetable oil
2 tbsp ginger, finely grated
2 tsp cumin seed
2 red chilli, deseeded and chopped
2 stalks lemongrass, finely chopped
2 cups vegetable stock
2 cups coconut milk
1 tbsp palm sugar
Coriander leaves to garnish

Bring the ingredients, except the coriander leaves, to a simmer and simmer until the potato is well cooked. Allow to cool a little before blending. Strain through a fine sieve and serve garnished with coriander leaves.

PUMPKIN AND ALMOND MILK SOUP

1 butternut pumpkin, peeled and diced
1 large onion, finely diced
3 cloves garlic, crushed
2 tbsp butter
500ml almond milk, plus extra for
     foam topping
500ml chicken stock
Several parsley or coriander sprigs
Salt and freshly ground black pepper

Gently sauté the onion, garlic and pumpkin in the butter. Add the almond milk, stock and herb of choice and simmer until the pumpkin is soft. Purée in a blender, Season to taste. Heat a little extra almond milk and with a milk frother create a froth to top soup.

SWEET POTATO CHIPS WITH CHILLI MINT SAUCE

Sweet potato
Oil for frying

Peel and cut the sweet potato into shoestring chips.
Deep fry until crisp. Drain well before serving.

Chilli mint sauce
1½ tbsp fresh chilli
2 cloves garlic, crushed
1 tbsp fresh mint
3 tbsp sugar
½ cup malt vinegar
Salt and pepper

Finely chop the herbs and mix with the other ingredients.

BABY POTATO WITH ASPARAGUS, TRUFFLE AND CRISP PROSCIUTTO

Baby potatoes
Sour cream
Parsley leaf
Asparagus spears, blanched
Truffle or truffle sauce
Prosciutto, crisped
Parmesan cheese

Boil the potatoes whole with the skin on. The skin
can be removed when cooked if necessary. Pipe some
sour cream onto the potato, add a leaf of parsley,
drizzle with truffle sauce and garnish with asparagus
spears and crisp prosciutto. Finish with a few shreds of
Parmesan cheese.

CRAB AND SWEETCORN CUSTARDS

50g butter
½ cup shallots, chopped
Pinch chilli flakes
2 tbsp chopped coriander
Zest of 1 lemon
3 cups corn kernels
2 cups cream
1 cup milk
5 egg yolks beaten
250g crab meat
1 tsp lemon juice
Salt and pepper

Sauté the shallots, chilli, coriander and lemon zest in
the butter. Add the corn, cream and milk and simmer
for about 5 minutes. Strain and add to the eggs, then
add the crab, salt and pepper and lemon juice. Mix well.
Place into small buttered cups or ramekins and cover
each cup with foil. Place in a bain-marie. and bake for
about 20 minutes or until set.

PARMESAN AND TRUFFLE CUSTARDS

330ml double cream
330ml milk
200g Parmesan cheese, grated
4 large eggs + 2 large egg yolks
Pinch sea salt,
Freshly ground white pepper
Truffle, finely diced

Parmesan tuiles
60g plain flour
90g flaked almonds
90g Parmesan cheese
45g melted butter
1 egg white

Heat the milk and cream to boiling point. Whisk the eggs and add the hot liquid. Add the Parmesan, diced truffle, (or garnish cooked custard with truffle) and season. Place into small buttered cups or ramekins and cover each dish with foil. Place in a bain-marie and bake for about 20 minutes in a moderate oven until just set. **Makes 12.**

Preheat the oven to 200C. Combine all the ingredients and roll the dough to a thin sheet. Cut into rounds and bake for about 8 minutes. While still warm bend over a rolling pin.

Variation
For simple tuiles spread finely grated Parmesan onto a parchment lined baking tray allowing plenty of space between each tuile and bake in a moderate oven until lightly golden.

BURNT LEEK AND CRAB CUSTARDS

1 leek, finely diced
1 tbsp butter
½ cup dry white wine
400ml cream
3 egg yolks, lightly beaten
100g crab meat
Salt and pepper

Cook the leek in the butter until dark golden. Add the wine and the cream and gently simmer. Season. Remove from the heat and strain. Whisk the eggs and add the hot liquid. Butter 8 ramekin dishes and place some crab meat into the base of each dish. ¾ fill the ramekins with the cream mixture and cover each dish with foil. Place in a bain-marie. Bake for about 20 minutes in a moderate oven until just set. Serve with Parmesan crisps and Melba toast. **Makes about 8.**

"There are no strangers here, only friends who haven't yet met!"

W.B. Yeats

FREE WiFi xxx

"*If the aunt of the vicar has never touched liquor, watch out when she finds the champagne.*"

Rudyard Kipling

7

PASTRY

Pastry is at the heart of all comfort food. It evokes memories of warm winter nights and wonderful home-cooked pies oozing with deliciousness. And today a perfect pastry can still steal the show. It is about coming up with contemporary flavour combinations, while not forgetting the traditional favourites. Each style of pastry is designed to complement its filling and give that special taste explosion with the first bite. Tart shells with beetroot relish or onion marmalade topped with goats curd and fresh herbs from the garden are always a winner.

Over the years I have tended to more often use puff pastry, so it is always on hand. It is delicate and light enough to enclose some lovely filling or to be transformed into fancy shaped savouries with a sprinkling of Parmesan, sesame seeds, sundried tomatoes, nigella seeds, almonds, olives, or walnuts.

WHOLEMEAL PASTRY

225g (1½ cups) wholemeal plain
    flour, sifted
½ tsp baking powder
125g butter
2 tbsp cold water
1 egg
A pinch of salt

In a food processor mix all the ingredients to make a firm dough. Cover and refrigerate for 30 minutes. Roll out and line mini muffin tins. The mixture will be quite soft and difficult to work with, but the result is worth it. Place the tins in the refrigerator or freezer for about 15 minutes. Line with parchment paper and baking beads and bake for approximately 7 minutes. Allow to cool before filling.

LARD PASTRY

600g (4 cups) plain flour
½ tsp salt
180g lard
70g butter
½ cup water

Sift the flour into a warm bowl with the salt. Bring the water to the boil with the lard and butter. Make a well in the flour and tip in the boiling liquid. Bring together with a wooden spoon until the mixture forms a dough. Roll out on a floured board to 5mm thickness and cut into triangles. Pinch the corners to make a shallow case, or line small tart tins. Place on a parchment lined baking tray and bake in a preheated 200C oven for about 30 minutes.

PARMESAN PASTRY

170g plain flour
85g butter
60g Parmesan cheese
Pinch of salt
2 egg yolks
Cold water

Blend the ingredients to resemble fine breadcrumbs. Add the egg yolks and enough water to bring the mixture together. Add a little salt. Knead for 5-6 minutes and rest the mixture before rolling. Refrigerate overnight before using.

CHOUX PASTRY

125ml milk
125ml water
100g butter, diced
½ tsp salt
1 tsp caster sugar
150g plain flour
4 eggs

Mix the milk, water, butter, salt and sugar in a saucepan and bring to the boil over a gentle heat. As soon as it boils remove from the heat and mix in the flour using a wooden spoon. Beat until smooth. Return the saucepan to the heat and stir the mixture continuously for a minute to dry out. Tip the mixture into a bowl and add the eggs one at a time whilst continuing to beat the mixture. The paste should be smooth and shiny. Spoon the mixture into a piping bag fitted with a 12mm-plain nozzle. Pipe 3cm-diameter mounds onto parchment paper, which has been moistened, on a baking tray. Bake for 15 minutes at 220C then reduce heat to 180C. At this time prick the pastries with a skewer and bake until golden and dry (about 5 minutes). Cool before filling.

YOGHURT PASTRY

400g self raising flour
80g chilled butter, cubed
¼ tsp salt
1 egg yolk
80ml plain Greek style yoghurt
2 tbsp cold water
1 tbsp cumin seeds
1 egg yolk, beaten to glaze
2 tbsp water

Process the flour, butter and salt to resemble breadcrumbs. Add the egg yolk, yoghurt, water and cumin seeds and combine well. Turn out and knead to a smooth dough. Cover and rest in the refrigerator for a couple of hours. When ready to use allow to stand at room temperature for about 15 minutes. Roll the pastry to about .5cm thick.

OATMEAL PASTRY

150g oats
100g wholemeal flour
Pinch sea salt
100g chilled butter, diced
1 egg
350g fine oatmeal
75g plain flour
1 ½ tsp baking powder
Pinch salt
115g butter
Milk, enough to make a stiff dough

Place the ingredients in a food processor and pulse until the mixture resembles fine breadcrumbs. Add a tablespoon or two of cold water to bring the mixture together. Roll into a ball and cover with clingfilm and rest in the refrigerator for a couple of hours before use. Excellent with a leek and Cheddar quiche filling or wild mushroom quiche mix.

SHORTCRUST PASTRY

250g plain flour
125g unsalted butter, chilled,
    finely diced
Pinch salt
1 egg

In a food processor process the flour, butter and salt until the mixture resembles breadcrumbs. Whisk the egg with a little chilled water. Add to the flour and butter mixture and blend until the mixture comes together. Turn out onto a floured surface and bring together. Wrap in clingfilm and refrigerate overnight until ready to use.

RICE FLOUR AND POLENTA PASTRY

75g rice flour
75g fine polenta
1 tsp xantham gum
Pinch of salt
150g butter, chilled
1 egg lightly beaten
2 tbsp water

In a food processor mix the flours and the butter until it resembles breadcrumbs. Add the egg, xantham gum and water. Bring the mixture together. Knead on a floured board until silky. Roll out and cut into rounds and line the tart tins. The mixture can be quite sticky and it is best to work with it whilst still chilled.

SESAME CUPS

310ml milk
225g plain flour
85g sugar
35g fine almond meal
10g salt
10g black sesame seeds
20g butter, melted
Pinch of bicarbonate of soda

Mix all the ingredients. Make in a waffle iron or a blini pan and shape when still warm.

BASIC QUICHE CUSTARD

1 ½ cups cream
3 large eggs
salt and pepper

Mix ingredients together. Suitable for most fillings, such as salmon and asparagus, and matching herbs.

CRAB WITH DICED FENNEL, PERSIMMON AND FINGER LIME TARTLETS

250g white crab meat
2 spring onions, julienned
1 small bulb fennel, finely julienned
3 non-astringent persimmons,
    julienned
1 tbsp lemon juice
2 tsp lemon infused oil plus extra
    for garnishing
Finger lime pulp

Mix all the salad ingredients together. Make a dressing with the lemon juice and lemon infused oil and mix. Fill the tart cases and garnish with the finger lime pulp.

Variation
Serve the crab with coriander and black garlic in spoons.

SWEET POTATO AND BLACK SESAME TWISTS

1 large sweet potato
1 tbsp kecap manis
1 tsp yasai fumi furikake
    (Japanese rice seasoning)
½ tsp shichimi togarashi
    (Japanese red pepper mix)
½ tsp salt
3 sheets ready rolled puff pastry
1 egg yolk mixed with a little milk
1 tbsp black sesame seeds

Bake the sweet potato whole with the skin on. Allow to cool. Remove the skin and mash with the Japanese seasonings, kecap manis and salt. Brush one side of the puff pastry with the egg wash and sprinkle with the black sesame seeds. Turn the pastry over onto parchment paper. Spread the sweet potato mixture onto half of the pastry. Fold in half to enclose the mixture and cut into fine strips. It is much easier to work with the pastry if it is very cold so put in the refrigerator in between each stage. Twist each strip and place on a parchment lined baking tray. Refrigerate for an hour or two before baking in a preheated oven at 190C until crisp.

LEEK PURĒE, SOFT BOILED QUAIL EGG AND TRUFFLE SAUCE TARTLETS

2 medium leeks, white part
    finely chopped
50g butter
75ml white wine
75ml cream
20 quail eggs
4cm shortcrust tart cases

Sweat the leek in the butter. Add the wine and reduce a little. Add the cream and cook until reasonably thick. Purée. Soft boil the quail eggs - 2 minutes and peel. Place a small amount of leek in each tart, top with a quail egg then spoon a little truffle sauce over each egg and serve at once.

Truffle sauce
50ml balsamic vinegar
50ml sherry vinegar
50ml ruby port
50ml truffle juice
50ml double cream
Cayenne pepper
A little salt

Place the vinegars, port and truffle juice in a small saucepan and reduce by three quarters by fast boiling. Stir in the cream and reduce to a thick syrupy consistency. Remove from the heat and work in the butter a little at a time. Season with salt and cayenne.

Variations
Top the leek purée with smoked trout.
Slow roast garlic cloves and shallots. Purée with cream and season. Top with soft boiled quail egg and fine julienne of fried leeks.

ROASTED PEPPER TARTLETS

Petite shortcrust tart cases
5 mixed peppers (capsicum)
2 shallots, finely diced
1 clove garlic crushed
2 whole eggs
4 egg yolks
150ml double cream
Salt and freshly ground black pepper

Cut each pepper into 4 and deseed. Place skin side up on a baking tray and place under a preheated grill until the skin is scorched. Remove from the grill and cover with a tea towel. When cool remove the skin. Gently sweat the shallots and garlic without browning. When cool mix with the eggs and purée. Finely slice about a third of the peppers. The remainder can be added to the shallot and garlic mixture and puréed. Add the cream and mix. Add the finely sliced peppers and season. Fill the tart shells and bake in a preheated 160C oven for about 10 minutes or until just set.

PROSCIUTTO PALMIERS

1 sheet puff pastry - 25cm x 25cm
3 tbsp honey mustard
100g thinly sliced prosciutto
1 cup finely grated Parmesan cheese
1 egg

Spread one side of the pastry with the mustard. Arrange the prosciutto evenly on top of the mustard then sprinkle with the Parmesan. Using a rolling pin press the cheese onto the prosciutto. Roll the opposite edges towards the centre of the pastry. Chill for an hour or two. Cut across into 1.25cm slices. Place on a parchment lined baking tray. Flatten the palmiers and refrigerate again for an hour. Beat the egg with 2 tsp water and brush the palmiers. Bake in a preheated 200C oven for about 10 minutes or until golden. **Makes about 20.**

Variations
Wild mushrooms cooked with thyme and seed mustard.
⅓ cup pesto with 1 cup finely grated Parmesan.

CARROT AND LEEK TARTS

1 medium leek, finely diced
2 medium carrots, finely grated
1-2 tbsp butter
150ml cream
2 whole eggs
3 egg yolks
1 tbsp dill
Salt and pepper
Tart cases

Gently sweat the leek and the carrots until soft. Mix the cream and eggs and add to the leek and carrot mixture along with the dill. Season. Fill the tart shells and cook in a preheated 160C oven until set.

ASPARAGUS AND HERBS IN RICE FLOUR AND POLENTA TARTLETS

50g each oregano, chives and basil,
    finely chopped
300g asparagus spears, stalks finely sliced
    (Reserve the tips to garnish the tart)
100ml cream
2 eggs
30g Parmesan
Salt and pepper
Rice flour and polenta pastry lined
    tart tins - uncooked

Blanch the asparagus and drain well. Add the herbs. Mix the cream, the eggs and Parmesan and add to the asparagus - keep the tips separate for garnishing. Season. Fill the tarts with the mixture, garnish with an asparagus tip and bake at 180C until the custard is set, and the pastry is cooked.

SLOW ROASTED TOMATO TART WITH ONION MARMALADE AND GOATS CURD

Cherry tomatoes, 3 per 4cm tart
A little olive oil
Basil leaves
Onion marmalade
Goats curd
4cm butter puff tart shells

Blanch the cherry tomatoes in boiling water then plunge into iced water. Peel. In a bowl toss them with a little olive oil and season. Drain and place on a parchment lined baking tray and dry out in a 50C oven for several hours. To assemble the tarts place a fresh basil leaf in the base of the tart, top with onion marmalade and a quenelle of goats curd.

WILD MUSHROOM GOUGERES

60g butter
500g mixed wild mushrooms,
    finely diced
40g shallot, finely diced
300ml double cream
2 tbsp parsley, finely chopped
Salt and freshly ground black pepper
1 quantity choux pastry, still warm
90g Emmental
Egg wash - 1 egg yolk and 1 tbsp milk
About 30g Parmesan, finely grated

Cook the mushrooms in the butter then add the cream. Cook for about 10 minutes then add the parsley. Season. Add the mushroom mixture and the cheese to the choux paste. Transfer the mixture to a piping bag with a 1cm nozzle and pipe small mounds, well spaced, onto a parchment lined baking try. Brush with the egg wash and sprinkle with the Parmesan. Bake for about 20 minutes in a preheated 180C oven. Serve immediately. **Makes about 40.**

SPINACH AND POACHED QUAIL EGG TARTLETS WITH HOLLANDAISE

Spinach, blanched and finely chopped
Quail eggs
Prosciutto, fine slices
Shortcrust tart cases
Hollandaise sauce

Cook the spinach with a little cream. Simmer until the cream has almost disappeared. Season. To crisp the prosciutto place on a parchment lined baking tray and dry out for about an hour in a very low oven - about 80C. Poach the quail eggs in a pan of water with a dash of vinegar which has been brought to a simmer. They will only take a couple of minutes to cook. To assemble the tarts spoon a little of the spinach mixture into the tart cases, top with the Hollandaise, then the quail egg and prosciutto and garnish. Serve immediately.

Hollandaise
1 egg yolk
125g clarified butter
1 tsp lemon juice

Whisk the yolk and 60ml water in a heatproof bowl over a saucepan of simmering water until the mixture holds ribbons. Add warm clarified butter in a thin stream, whisking continuously until sauce is emulsified, whisk in the lemon juice and season.

Variation
Fill tart cases with mushroom purée and top with soft boiled quail egg and Hollandaise.

WILD MUSHROOM TARTLETS

250g wild mushrooms, finely diced
50g butter
1 medium onion, finely chopped
2 garlic cloves, crushed
1 tsp dried thyme
Salt and pepper
1 cup chicken stock
2 tbsp Madeira or sherry
½ cup double cream
Juice of ½ lemon
Fresh parsley
Ready made tart shells

Sauté the onion and garlic in the butter taking care not to burn them. Add the mushrooms and sauté for 5 minutes. Remove the onions, garlic and mushrooms from the pan and add 1 tbsp flour to the pan juices. Cook until lightly browned. Add the stock, lemon juice, cream and thyme to the pan and reduce to half by boiling. Add the mushrooms and Madeira or sherry to the sauce. Fill ready made tart cases or top brioche toasts with the mushroom mixture and garnish with flat leaf parsley.

CHICKEN AND ROCKET SAUSAGE ROLLS WITH SESAME SEEDS

500g chicken and rocket or chicken
and chive sausages
2 x 25cm x 25cm ready roll puff pastry
sheets
1 egg, lightly beaten
Sesame seeds

Brush the puff pastry with the lightly beaten egg. Cut each puff pastry sheet in half. Remove the skins from the sausages and place about 1 ½ sausages on each sheet and roll. Seal each end of the rolls. Brush the roll with more egg and sprinkle with seeds. Place on a baking sheet and refrigerate until the pastry has become firm again (or even freeze). When ready to cook cut each roll into 6 or 7 and bake in a preheated 220C oven for 20 -30 minutes until the pastry is puffed and golden. Serve with a good tomato relish or chilli plum sauce. **Makes 24-28 rolls.**

AUBERGINE TARTLETS TOPPED WITH DRAINED YOGHURT

200g mixed cherry tomatoes
200g aubergine, finely diced
Pinch ground cumin
½ medium sized red onion, finely diced
½ red chilli, finely chopped
1 clove garlic, crushed
½ tbsp fresh mint, finely chopped
½ tbsp fresh coriander, finely chopped
Salt and freshly ground pepper
Olive oil

Skin the tomatoes and place on a parchment lined baking tray. Toss the aubergine in the oil and spread out on another lined baking tray. Put both the tomatoes and aubergine into a preheated 180C oven. Cook until the aubergines are golden and the tomatoes have softened. Cool slightly, dice the tomatoes if they are too big. Heat some olive oil in a frying pan over a medium heat. Add the onions, garlic and chilli and sauté. Add the cumin then add the tomatoes and aubergine. Mix well then add the herbs. Season to taste. Refrigerating overnight brings out the flavours. Bring to room temperature before serving.

Lard pastry tart cases
Fresh coriander and fresh mint,
to garnish
Drained yoghurt, to garnish
Olives to garnish, optional
Flat leaf parsley to garnish

Fill the tart cases with the aubergine filling, top with the drained yoghurt and garnish with the parsley.

Drained yoghurt
200g tub Greek style yoghurt or
goats milk yoghurt

Place the yoghurt in a muslin lined sieve and drain at least overnight. Make a quenelle to top the tarts.

POLENTA CUPS WITH CHILLI CON CARNE

6 tbsp butter
100g Philadelphia cream cheese
1 cup plain flour
½ cup fine polenta
Pinch of salt

Cream the butter and cream cheese. Add the flour and polenta slowly. Roll into balls and line patty tins. Chill for at least 1 hour. Bake blind for about 20 minutes in 200C oven. Fill with chilli con carne for serving.

Chilli con carne
2 tbsp olive oil
1 onion, finely chopped
2 garlic cloves, chopped
2 tsp chilli powder   ) or 1-2 tsp
1 tsp ground cumin   ) Mexican
1 tsp ground coriander) chilli powder
1 bay leaf
2 tbsp plain flour
500g good beef mince
500g ripe tomatoes, peeled, chopped
2 tbsp tomato paste
400g can red kidney beans,
    drained, rinsed
1 bunch coriander, leaves and
    stems chopped

Cook the onion and the garlic in the oil, add the spice and meat and cook until browned. Add the tomatoes, tomato paste, and beans and stir until well combined. Add a little water if necessary. Bring to the boil then reduce to a simmer and cook until the meat is tender and the moisture has been absorbed. Season. Add some chopped coriander leaves.

Variation: Make corn cups using:
125g masa harina/maize flour
½ tsp salt
150ml warm water

LEEK AND HAM CROISSANTS

Ready rolled puff pastry sheets
2 tbsp butter
½ cup leek, finely diced
75g cooked ham, finely diced
½ tsp sage, finely chopped
Salt and pepper
Beaten egg to glaze
Caraway, poppy or sesame seeds
    to sprinkle

Melt the butter and sweat the leek until soft. Add the ham and sage and season. Cook until all the liquid has been absorbed. Cut the pastry into triangles measuring 10cm across the base. Place a little filling at the base of each triangle and roll up. Twist the ends around to meet to form croissants. Place on a parchment paper lined baking tray. Rest for 30 minutes in the refrigerator. Brush with the beaten egg and sprinkle with the seeds. Bake in a preheated 200C oven for about 20 minutes. Serve warm.

GOATS CURD CIGARS MADE WITH BRIK PASTRY

Brik pastry
Butter, melted
Goats curd

Cut the brik pastry to the size you require and brush each sheet lightly with the melted butter. Roll each sheet around a 3cm diameter metal cylinder to form a tube. Bake in a preheated oven until golden. When cooked and slightly cool remove gently from the cylinder. Cool completely before piping in the goats curd. Serve as soon as you have filled them.

SESAME TUBES FILLED WITH SMOKED SALMON AND TOPPED WITH CAVIAR

160ml milk
2 tbsp cornflour
100g plain flour
40g sugar
20g almond meal
Pinch of salt
5-10g sesame seeds
10g vegetable oil
Pinch of bicarbonate of soda

Mix all the ingredients together and allow to stand several hours before cooking. Cook in a waffle iron if you have one, or as you would for a pancake in a blini pan. Dilute the batter if it is too thick. The pancakes should be thin. As soon as they are cooked trim the edges and roll around a 3cm metal cylinder. Completely dry out in the oven before filling.

250g Regal wood roasted salmon fillet
    with spices
70g mascarpone
Mayonnaise to adjust texture
1 spring onion, finely chopped
Several dill sprigs, finely chopped

The Regal salmon has a soft texture. Mix with the other ingredients. Adjust the texture with mayonnaise so that the mixture is able to be piped into the tubes. Remove the scales from the skin and cut into strips. Dry out in the oven and use as a garnish. To serve add a small dot of mayonnaise, caviar and the dried out salmon skin.

SPINACH AND WALNUT TURNOVERS WITH TAHINI SAUCE

1.5 kg spinach, washed and
    roughly chopped
40g butter
3 onions, finely diced
75g walnuts, finely chopped
½ tsp ground allspice
½ tsp ground cinnamon
Salt and pepper
Sheets of ready rolled butter puff pastry
1 egg yolk

Melt the butter in a pan and sauté the onions until soft. Add the spinach and cook until the spinach is dry. Mix in the nuts, spices and seasoning. Cut the puff pastry into circles and fill each circle with the spinach filling. Fold over and pinch the edges together. Brush with the egg yolk. Bake in a preheated 220C for about 30 minutes. Serve with the tahini sauce.

Tahini sauce
90ml tahini
2 tbsp sunflower oil
90-120ml thick plain yoghurt
Lemon juice to taste

Blend all the sauce ingredients together.

LAMB AND SPINACH PASTRIES

300g lean lamb, minced
4 shallots, finely chopped
2 cloves garlic, crushed
1 Granny Smith apple,
    peeled and grated
½ tsp ground cinnamon
½ tsp ground nutmeg
½ tsp ground ginger
Small bunch of coriander, finely chopped
1 tbsp pomegranate molasses
150g pine nuts, roughly chopped
200g baby spinach leaves
Yoghurt based pastry, rolled and
    cut into 6cm rounds.

In a bowl combine the first 10 ingredients. Season to taste. Blanch the spinach in some boiling water. Drain and squeeze dry. Chop and add to the meat. Mix well. To assemble, place a spoonful of the lamb mixture in the centre of the pastry. Pinch the sides together. Brush the pastry with the egg mixture and bake in a 220C oven for about 12-15 minutes or until golden brown. **Makes about 24.**

YUFKA PASTRY FOR BOREK

450g (3 cups) plain flour
55ml water
½ tsp salt
225g butter
2 eggs
1 beaten egg with 1 tbsp water to glaze

Sift the flour and add the salt. Work in the butter then add the 2 eggs. Add the water gradually until the dough forms a soft ball and comes away from the side of the bowl. Rest in a cool place, covered, for several hours. Roll the dough out on a floured board as thinly as possible. Cut into strips, place the filling in the centre, fold over and pinch the edges together. Glaze with the beaten egg. Place on a parchment lined baking tray and bake in a 180C oven until golden - about 45 minutes.

SPINACH BOREK

225g frozen chopped spinach
1 onion, finely chopped
Vegetable oil
2 tbsp pine nuts or chopped walnuts
1-2 tbsp raisins
Salt and pepper
1 quantity of yufka pastry, filo pastry or
    a yoghurt based flaky pastry

Defrost and drain the spinach. Sauté the onion in the oil until soft. Add the spinach and cook until the moisture has been absorbed. Lightly toast the pine nuts or walnuts. Add with the raisins to the spinach. Season and mix well.

SWEET POTATO AND SPRING ONION BOREK

2 large sweet potatoes
10g butter
6 spring onions, finely sliced
½ tsp paprika
½ tbsp nigella seeds
Melted butter to brush the pastry
    if using filo
1 egg yolk, beaten
1 tsp nigella seeds
1 quantity of yufka pastry or filo pastry

In a preheated oven bake the sweet potato whole. Allow to cool and peel. Melt the butter and add to the sweet potato in a bowl. Add the spring onions, paprika and nigella seeds. Wrap in filo, or yufka pastry. Glaze the wrapped boreks with the beaten egg and sprinkle with nigella seeds. Bake in a preheated 190C oven for about 12-15 minutes.

TUNA AND PARMESAN PUFFS

½ cup water
60g butter
¾ cup plain flour
2 eggs, lightly beaten
¼ cup Parmesan

Heat the water and the butter until melted. Off the heat add the plain flour and beat until the mixture leaves the side of the pan. Add the beaten egg a little at a time then add the Parmesan. Transfer the mixture to a piping bag and pipe onto a damp parchment lined baking tray. Allow plenty of space between each puff. Bake at 220C for about 12-14 minutes. When cool make a slit in the side and pipe in the tuna filling.

1 x 198g tin tuna chunks in brine, drained
6 tbsp good mayonnaise
1 tbsp parsley, finely chopped
Salt and pepper

Blend the tuna, mayonnaise, and parsley together. Season. Transfer to a piping bag and fill the Parmesan puffs.

CHEESE PUFFS

1 cup plain flour
1 tsp baking powder
½ tsp salt
½ tsp dry English mustard
2 egg yolks, beaten
½ cup milk
1 cup Cheddar, grated
2 egg whites, beaten to soft peak
Oil for frying

Mix the flour, baking powder and salt together. Add the mustard, egg yolks, milk and Cheddar. Fold in the beaten egg whites. Drop small balls of the mixture into hot oil. Serve immediately.

PUFF PASTRY SAVOURIES

Ready rolled puff pastry sheets
1 egg yolk, beaten
Toppings such as Parmesan,
    sundried tomatoes,
    nigella seeds, almonds,
    olives, walnuts etc

Brush the pastry sheet with the egg yolk and cut into various shapes. Be creative with the toppings and bake in a preheated 200C oven.

GOATS CHEESE CAKES

2 x 20 x 20cm sheets ready rolled
    puff pastry
3 tbsp butter, melted
1 tsp poppy seeds
1 tsp sesame seeds
250g soft goats cheese
100g Philadelphia cream cheese
150ml double cream
1 small tsp gelatine
3 tbsp finely diced and sautéed red onion
Parsley or chives, finely chopped,
    optional
Caramelised onion marmalade to top
Micro herbs to serve

Bake the pastry sheets on a parchment lined baking tray until crisp and golden. When cool reduce to crumbs in a food processor with the poppy seeds and the sesame seeds. Add enough butter to bring the mixture together. Press into the base of a flat based and sided tin which has been lined with parchment paper. Mix the gelatine in a little boiling water and stir until completely dissolved. Mix the cheeses and double cream together until smooth. Add the sautéed onion, herbs and gelatine. Mix well then pour into the pastry lined tin. Chill for several hours in the refrigerator. When set cut into desired size and shapes and top with caramelised onion marmalade and micro herbs.

CROXETTI WITH MUSHROOM JELLY

Croxetti -4cm coin shaped pasta
Parmesan, finely grated

Boil the croxetti until al dente. Place on a parchment lined baking tray, sprinkle with Parmesan and place in a hot oven until the Parmesan is golden.

Mushroom jelly
2 tsp truffle butter - optional
½ leek, white part only, finely chopped
200g mixed mushrooms
100ml Noilly Prat
150ml chicken or vegetable stock
150ml double cream
Salt and freshly ground black pepper
Gelatine
Parsley to garnish

Gently sauté the leek and the mushrooms in the truffle butter. Add the Noilly Prat, stock and cream and simmer for about 15 minutes. Remove from the heat and allow to cool a little. Pureé in a blender until smooth. Dissolve the gelatine and add to the pureéd mushrooms. Pour the mixture into a flat dish so that the jelly is at least 1.5cm deep. Allow to cool and refrigerate until set. Cut to fit between the croxetti. Assemble and garnish with parsley.

"*I am easily satisfied with the best.*"

Winston Churchill, on Champagne

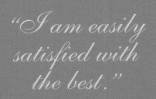

8

THE CHEESEBOARD &
ITS FRIENDS

The arrival of the cheeseboard can indicate two things: last drinks or, joy of joys, the opening of a special bottle of red wine and another couple of hours of chat. When time is not an issue and the conversation is flowing, this is the moment to produce a generous selection of cheeses and other tempting treats – especially biscuits, wafers, and breads to complement the board.

Choose the cheese thoughtfully and offer plenty of variety. A classic soft French D'Affinois, some Chevré, Roblochon, and the old English Cheddars and Stilton.

It is a great finale to any occasion.

CHEESE BISCUITS

250g plain flour
200g butter, softened
225g strong Cheddar cheese, or
    vintage Gouda, grated
Optional flavours such as chilli,
    black pepper, rosemary, thyme- or
    roll in a smoked paprika or
    pink pepper mix

Combine flour, cheese and butter in a food processor and process until the ingredients come together in a ball. Do not overwork the mixture. Transfer the dough to a floured board and roll into several cylindrical shapes. Coat with the selected flavours. Wrap with clingfilm and refrigerate or freeze until required. When ready to bake, preheat the oven to 180°C. Slice the dough into 1 cm thick rounds and bake for about 10 minutes. This mixture does freeze very well. **Makes about 70.**

PARMESAN AND OLIVE BISCUITS

100g grated Parmesan
100g butter
100g plain flour
40g Kalamata olives

Process the cheese, butter and flour in a food processor until the mixture resembles breadcrumbs. Add the chopped olives and combine. Roll into balls and flatten. Place on a parchment lined baking tray and bake for about 8-10 minutes at 180C. **Makes about 30.**

ANCHOVY WAFERS

130g plain flour
125g chilled butter
125g strong mature Cheddar cheese
2 tbsp fresh marjoram, finely chopped
100g anchovies in olive oil, drained
    and cut into half lengthwise
Black pepper

Mix the flour, butter, Cheddar and marjoram and black pepper to a soft dough. Mould into a flat rectangle and refrigerate for one hour. Cut into fingers and place an anchovy fillet on each finger. Cook for 8 minutes in a preheated 200C oven. **Makes about 50.**

PESTO OR GARLIC FLAVOURED FLAT BREADS

1 packet of tortillas
Olive oil
1 jar or tube of pesto or garlic purée

Brush the tortillas with olive oil and spread with either pesto or garlic purée. Black pepper goes well with the garlic purée. Dry out in a very slow oven. They must not brown as they will become bitter.

CAPERBERRIES IN CHEESE PASTRY

250g vintage Cheddar, grated
50g butter
85g plain flour
Pinch of cayenne pepper
25 caperberries with stalks intact

Process the cheese, butter, flour and cayenne pepper until the mixture resembles breadcrumbs. Bring the mixture together and chill for an hour. Drain the caperberries. Roll pastry to about 1 cm thickness and cut 4 cm rounds. Top each round with a caperberry. Fold pastry to encase the caperberry leaving the stalk exposed. Chill the balls for an hour before placing on a parchment lined baking tray. Bake in a moderately hot oven for about 15 minutes or until lightly browned. Cool before serving. **Makes 25.**

Variation
Try wrapping stuffed olives with the cheese pastry.

ROSEMARY AND PARMESAN STRAWS

1 sheet ready rolled butter puff pastry
⅓ cup finely grated Parmesan
1 tbsp rosemary, finely chopped
½ tsp freshly ground black pepper

Brush one side of the pastry with water. In a bowl mix the cheese, rosemary and pepper and spread on the pastry. Slice the pastry into strips and place on a parchment lined baking tray. Bake in a preheated 190C oven for about 10 minutes, or until golden. **Makes about 20.**

PARMESAN GRISSINI

1 tsp active dried yeast
A pinch of caster sugar
1 tbsp olive oil
60g Parmesan, grated
1 tsp sea salt
250g strong flour

Pour 170ml warm water into a small bowl. Sprinkle with the yeast and the sugar and leave in a warm place for 10 minutes or until foamy. Stir in the olive oil. Put the flour in a large bowl and add the Parmesan and salt and stir well. Pour in the yeast mixture and stir until a dough forms. Turn out onto a lightly floured surface and knead for 5 minutes until smooth and elastic. Place the dough in a large oiled bowl turning to coat in oil. Cover with clingfilm and leave to rise in a warm place for about an hour or until doubled in size. Lightly grease two baking trays. Knock back the dough and turn out onto a lightly floured work surface and cut in half. Roll out one piece of dough to form a 20 x 16 cm rectangle then cut it into 16 strips about 1 cm wide. Gently roll each strip to form a 22 -24 cm long stick. Place on one of the baking trays. Repeat with the second piece of dough. Bake in a 200C preheated oven for 17-20 minutes, or until golden and crisp. Cool on a wire rack.

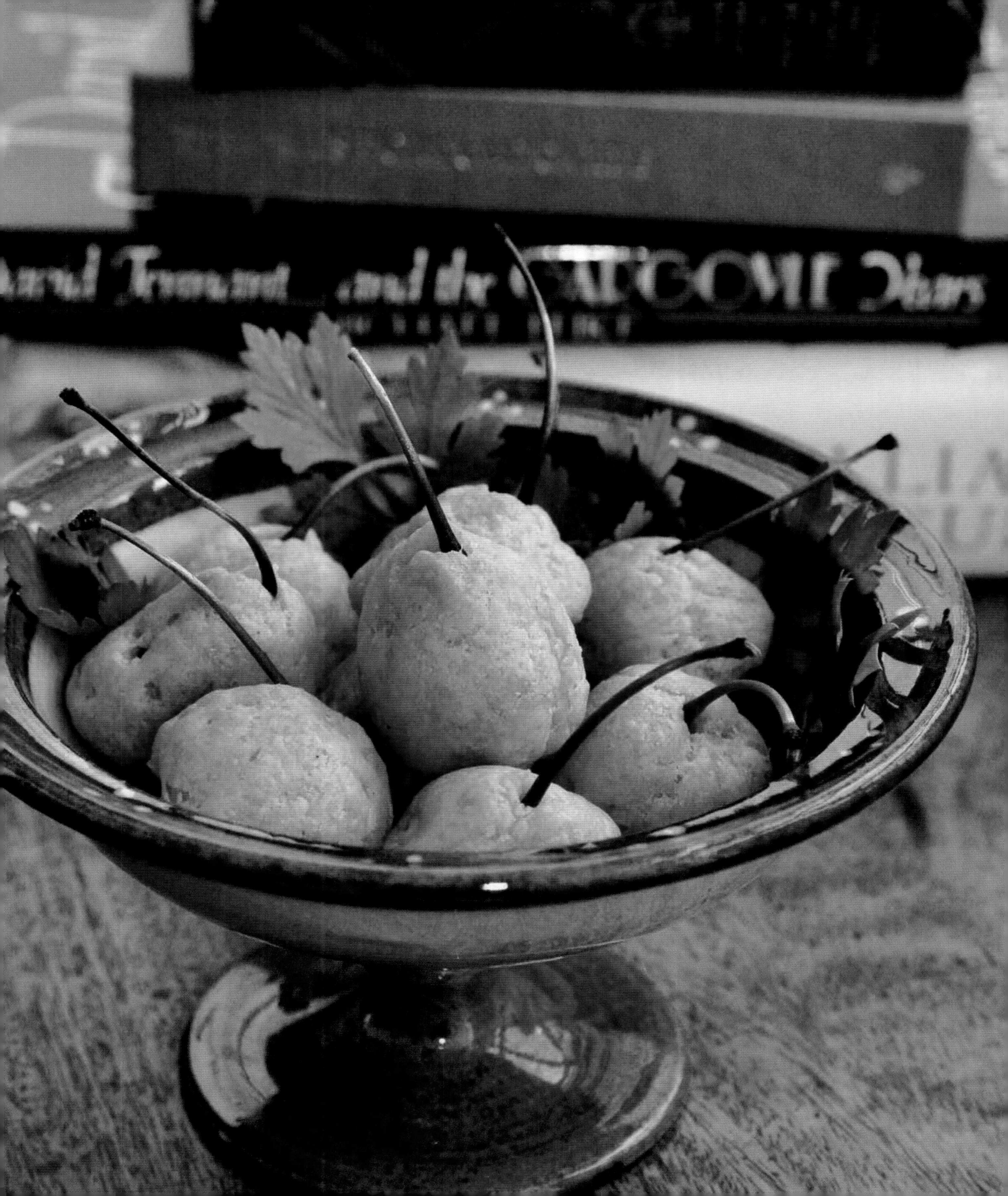

ROSEMARY AND NIGELLA SEED WAFERS

85g grated Cheddar
60g grated Parmesan
80g butter
110g plain flour
1 tsp Worcestershire sauce
2 tsp rosemary, finely chopped
1 tsp nigella or mustard seeds

Process the cheeses, flour, butter and Worcestershire sauce in a food processor until the mixture resembles breadcrumbs. Add the rosemary and seeds and combine. Bring the mixture together on a floured board. Wrap in clingfilm and refrigerate for at least an hour. Roll out to 1 mm thickness. Cut into desired shapes or tear into triangles and bake on baking parchment at 190C for about 8 minutes. **Makes about 40.**

CRISPY CORN WAFERS

125g polenta
¼ tsp chilli powder
350ml boiling water
25g melted butter
½ tsp salt

Mix all the ingredients together. Pour spoonfuls onto a heated baking tray making sure they are well spaced. Bake for 15-20 minutes in a preheated 200C oven.

OATCAKES

3 cups rolled oats
135g wholemeal plain flour
60g butter
⅓ cup brown sugar
¼ cup milk
¼ cup golden syrup
150g Mascarpone Reale to serve or
     Blue Costello

Process the rolled oats in a food processor for about 1 minute. Combine with flour and a good pinch of salt. Add the butter and process until the mixture resembles fine breadcrumbs. Mix in the sugar. Heat the milk and golden syrup. Add to the rolled oats mixture and mix to a firm dough. Divide into 4 equal portions and roll each to a 3mm thickness and mark into wedges or cut into 4.5cm discs. Place on a parchment lined baking tray and bake at 180C for about 10 minutes or until lightly golden. Cool on the tray. Serve with the cheese.

Variation
350g fine oatmeal
75g plain flour
1 ½ tsp baking powder
Pinch salt
115g butter
Milk (enough to make a stiff dough)

Process as above and serve with cheese.

WALNUT AND BLACK PEPPER OATCAKES

25g walnuts, blitzed in a food processor
65g medium oatmeal
65g plain flour
½ tsp coarsely ground black pepper
¼ tsp bicarbonate of soda
¼ tsp salt
40g butter, melted
1 tsp runny honey

Mix all the dry ingredients with the walnuts in a bowl. Add the melted butter and the honey and a tablespoon of water and mix to a soft dough. Roll out to 3-5mm thickness and cut with a 4.5 cm cutter and place on a parchment lined baking tray. Bake for about 10 minutes in a 190C preheated oven. These are excellent with fresh goats cheese, or a blue cheese. **Makes about 20.**

WALNUT BUTTER ON SODA BREAD WITH PARSLEY AND BLACK GARLIC

Soda bread
Black garlic
Flat leaf parsley
Walnut halves to garnish

Slice the bread to toast thickness and toast under a grill on one side only. Spread with the walnut butter on the untoasted side and cut into serving size fingers. Top with a leaf of parsley, a clove of black garlic and a walnut half. Return to the grill and cook for only a couple of minutes making sure not to burn. Serve warm.

Wholemeal soda bread

250g wholemeal flour
125g plain flour
1 tsp bicarbonate of soda
1 tsp salt
300ml buttermilk or natural yoghurt

Line a 500g loaf tin with parchment paper and preheat the oven to 200C. Place the flours together in a large bowl and add the bicarbonate of soda and salt. Make a well in the centre and pour in the buttermilk or natural yoghurt. Mix well and add liquid if necessary to give a soft drop consistency. Spoon the mixture into the prepared tin and bake for about 40-45 minutes until well risen and sounds hollow when tapped on the bottom. Cool on a rack.

Walnut butter

100g walnuts
250g butter

Blend the walnuts and butter together to create a reasonably fine spread.

BAKED PAVE D'AFFINOIS WRAPPED IN LEEK AND TOPPED WITH ROASTED ALMONDS

⅓ cup whisky or rum
½ cup brown sugar
Couple of handfuls walnuts or almonds
Pave d'Affinois or Brie

Mix the whisky and the sugar and allow to sit for a day at least. Wrap the cheese with the spring onion. Cut a circle in the top of the cheese and drizzle in the whisky mixture. Top with the nuts and bake for about 10 minutes at 180C. Serve with lavosh or grissini.

CUMIN AND PISTACHIO BISCOTTI

110g plain flour
½ tsp cumin seeds
1 tbsp shelled pistachios, chopped
10ml olive oil
10g caster sugar
4 egg whites

Combine the flour in a bowl with cumin, pistachios, oil, sugar, a pinch of salt and freshly ground black pepper to taste. Beat the egg whites until stiff peaks form and fold into the flour mixture. Spoon into a small parchment lined loaf tin and bake at 160C for 45 minutes. When cool slice thinly and place on a parchment line baking tray and bake at 190C for 5-10 minutes or until lightly toasted. Cool on a wire rack. **Makes about 18-20 biscotti.**

POPPY SEED WAFERS

125g cold butter, diced
230g wholemeal self raising flour
190ml buttermilk
125g poppy seeds

Blend the butter and flour until it resembles breadcrumbs. Slowly add the buttermilk and mix until smooth. Remove to a floured board and roll into a sausage shape 3cm in diameter. Refrigerate for an hour. Slice rounds from the roll. Sprinkle poppy seeds onto the floured surface and roll wafer out into a thin disc. Bake at 190C for 8-10 minutes or until lightly browned. Cool and store in an airtight container. **Makes 16.**

WALNUT SHORTBREAD FOR BLUE CHEESE

125g butter
¼ cup icing sugar
½ cup rice flour
½ heaped cup of walnut pieces
½ cup wholemeal plain flour
Blue or White Costello cheese for topping
Dried figs
Flat leaf parsley

In a food processor cream the butter and the icing sugar. Add the walnuts and mix until the walnuts are finely chopped. Add the rice flour and plain flour and mix gently. Refrigerate for an hour before rolling to 5mm thickness. Cut into the desired shapes. Bake at 160C in a preheated oven for about 30 minutes. Do not overcook. When cool top with cheese and a slice of fig and parsley.

MACADAMIA NUT BISCUITS FOR CHEESE

120g rice flour
80g macadamia nuts
30g coconut flour
½ tsp baking powder
½ tsp salt
½ tsp garlic powder
3 tbsp butter, chopped
2 eggs

Process in a food processor the rice flour, macadamia nuts, coconut flour, baking powder, salt and garlic powder until the mixture resembles breadcrumbs. Add the butter and the eggs and process until the mixture comes together. The mixture will be quite sticky. Refrigerate for an hour or so. Divide the mixture into two and roll out very thinly between two pieces of parchment paper. Cut into desired shapes and bake on the parchment paper in a preheated 180C oven until golden. Do not allow to overcook.

GOATS CHEESE BISCUITS

100g Parmesan, grated
50g firm goats cheese, grated
150g butter
150g plain flour
½ tsp caraway seeds or dried thyme
    or pink peppercorns, crushed
Freshly ground black pepper

Process the cheeses, butter, flour, and black pepper in a food processor until a dough forms. Add the caraway seeds, thyme or pink peppercorns and mix. Form into a log and wrap in clingfilm and refrigerate for at least an hour until firm. Cut into 1 cm thick slices and place biscuits 4 cm apart on a greased baking tray. Sprinkle with a few extra seeds or thyme and bake at 180C for 15 minutes or until crisp and golden. Cool on trays. **Makes about 40.**

CARAMELISED FIG AND BLUE CHEESE ON SEEDED SODA BREAD

Seeded soda bread
Soft blue cheese such as Blue Costello
Fresh figs
Brown sugar
Fig conserve
Prosciutto
Sour cream
Baby salad leaves to garnish

Cut the figs into quarters, sprinkle with the brown sugar and caramelise under a hot grill for a couple of minutes. Slice the soda bread into slices then cut with a 4.5cm cutter. Toast lightly. Cut the prosciutto into thin strips and crisp in a low oven. To assemble spread the soda bread with a little sour cream, then add some fig conserve, a wedge of blue cheese, prosciutto and top with the caramelised fig. Garnish with micro herbs.

Seeded soda bread
200g wholemeal flour
200g plain flour, sifted
1 tsp bicarbonate of soda
1 tsp salt
25g pumpkin seeds
25g sunflower seeds
1 tbsp linseeds
300ml buttermilk
1 tbsp treacle
1 tbsp sunflower oil

Line a 500g loaf tin with parchment paper and preheat the oven to 200C. Place the flours together in a large bowl and add the bicarbonate of soda, salt and most of the nuts. Reserve some of the nuts for the topping. Make a well in the centre and pour in the buttermilk, treacle and sunflower oil. Stir the mixture together until well blended, adding a little more buttermilk if necessary to give a soft drop consistency. Spoon the mixture into the prepared tin and sprinkle over the reserved seeds. Bake for about 40-45 minutes until well risen and sounds hollow when tapped on the bottom. Cool on a rack.

CHEESE AND NUT BALLS

Pear and almond paste, quince
    paste or fig paste
Brie or Camembert cheese
Almonds or pistachios, or mixed nuts,
    finely chopped

Cut the paste into small cubes. Remove the rind from the cheese and roll a small piece around the cube of paste then roll in the chopped nuts. Refrigerate before serving.

MARINATED YOGHURT BALLS WITH HERBS

1 cup Greek yoghurt
Mixed fresh herbs of choice such
    as parsley, oregano, chives, basil
Good olive oil

Place the yoghurt in a muslin cloth, tie up and drain overnight. Roll into balls and place in a jar with the chopped herbs and olive oil. Marinate for a couple of days before using.

"There comes a time in every woman's life when the only thing that helps is a glass of champagne."

Bette Davis

9

SWEET ENDINGS

Who can resist a final glass of bubbles? Chilled and freshly popped, all that it needs is a sweet delicacy to complete the bliss: a petite raspberry and chocolate pot, or an almond tart.

I have selected an eclectic mix of dessert recipes that most find irresistible. Some are perfect for morning or afternoon tea (even without Champagne!) and others provide the 'wow' factor at the end of a dinner party. There are some that have stood the test of time and some new, lighter dishes that are becoming increasingly popular today.

ALMOND TARTS

Almond pastry
225g plain flour
85g ground almonds
110g caster sugar
170g butter
2 egg yolks
½ tsp vanilla essence

Rub the butter, egg yolks and vanilla into the dry ingredients. Rest the pastry for a couple of hours before rolling.

Filling
1 egg
1 egg yolk
4 tbsp caster sugar
125g ground almonds
3 tbsp double cream
A few drops of vanilla
10 blanched almonds to garnish

Beat the eggs with the sugar until thick and light. Stir in the ground almonds, cream and vanilla. Fill the tart cases to ¾ full. Bake for 15 minutes in a preheated 190C oven. Remove from the oven and top with a blanched almond. Continue to cook until the filling is set.

Variation
Put some berry jam on the base of the tart shell before filling.

ALMOND DROPS

1 cup ground almonds
1 cup icing sugar
¼ cup orange blossom water
Pistachio nuts, chopped to top

Mix the ground almonds, icing sugar and just enough orange blossom water to make a stiff paste. Knead until smooth. Shape into small balls and roll in the icing sugar. Decorate with chopped pistachios.

LEBANESE ALMOND BISCUITS

Syrup
250g caster sugar
¾ cup water
2 tsp lemon juice
1 tbsp orange flower water

Heat the sugar and water until dissolved. Add half the lemon juice and simmer until the syrup is thick enough to coat the back of the spoon. Add remaining lemon juice and orange flower water and simmer another couple of minutes. Cool and refrigerate before using.

Biscuits
5 cups medium grain semolina
2 ½ cups caster sugar
125g butter, melted
1 cup milk
200g blanched almonds

Mix the semolina, sugar, butter and milk. Spread evenly on a parchment lined shallow baking tray. Cut into diamond shapes and place a blanched almond in each diamond. Bake in a preheated 180C oven for about 30 minutes or until golden. Pour over the cold syrup and leave until it reaches room temperature before serving.

RASPBERRY OR PRALINE TOPPED CHOCOLATE POTS

Praline
½ cup caster sugar
2 tbsp cold water
¼ cup slivered almonds

Ready made chocolate pots
Chocolate ganache
Fresh raspberries or praline

Chocolate ganache
200ml whipping cream
200g best quality dark chocolate
25g liquid glucose
50g butter, diced and chilled

Combine the sugar and the water in a saucepan over low heat. Cook for a couple of minutes stirring until the sugar has dissolved. Increase the heat and bring to the boil. Do not stir. Cook until golden. Remove from the heat, add the almonds and pour onto a parchment lined baking tray. Cool well before pulsing to top the chocolate pots.

Bring the cream to the boil in a saucepan. Remove from the heat and add the chocolate and glucose a little at a time stirring with a whisk to make a smooth cream. Whisk in the butter a cube at a time. Fill the chocolate pots or larger tarts made with the lemon pastry. Top with a raspberry or garnish with praline.

Note: In the event of having some leftover ganache, stir through some mixed nuts, mixed fruit or chopped crystallised ginger and roll into balls.

PRALINE PALMIERS AND TWISTS

Ready rolled puff pastry sheets
1 egg lightly beaten
Praline*
Icing sugar for dusting

*For the Praline see recipe
    page 178

For the palmiers, place the pastry sheet on a floured board. Sprinkle with praline then fold the pastry in three and roll out again. Sprinkle with a little more praline fold in three again and roll out. Fold in three again and chill for 30 minutes. Heat the oven to 200C. Roll the pastry to 1cm then roll up to form a log. Slice into 1 cm slices. Place on a parchment lined baking tray and bake for about 10 minutes. For the twists, brush the pastry with a little beaten egg and sprinkle with some praline mix. Cut into 2 cm strips. Taking both ends of the strips twist into shape and place on a parchment lined baking tray, pressing both ends down firmly. Bake in a preheated 200C oven for about 8-10 minutes.

WHITE CHOCOLATE TARTS WITH RASPBERRIES

Lemon pastry, or ready made cases
Small basil leaves
Pink peppercorns
Raspberries
Spun sugar to garnish

Roll out the pastry and line 4.5cm tart tins. Bake blind in a preheated 180C oven. Cool before filling. Line with a small basil leaf, add a couple of pink peppercorns before filling with the white chocolate cream, and topping with raspberries. Garnish with some spun sugar.

White chocolate cream
375g white chocolate
3 egg yolks
750ml whipping cream

Melt the white chocolate in a double boiler. Beat in 45ml of hot water and the egg yolks one at a time. Remove from the heat and allow to cool. Whip the cream and fold into the chocolate mixture.

Lemon pastry
1 egg
85g sugar
285g plain flour
Pinch of salt
145g butter
Zest of 1 lemon

In a food processor process the egg and sugar until well combined. Add the flour and salt and mix until the mixture resembles breadcrumbs. Add the butter and lemon zest and mix to form a dough. Wrap and set aside before rolling.

TOFFEE NUT TARTS

About 20 4 cm tart shells
200g mix of fruit and nuts, (pine nuts,
    pistachios, slivered almonds, diced
    macadamia nuts, dried cranberries,
    sultanas, citrus peel or diced
    dried fruit
50g unsalted butter
50g golden syrup
50g caster sugar
Icing sugar for dusting

Melt the golden syrup, caster sugar and butter in a saucepan. Bring slowly to the boil and simmer for 2 minutes until a light toffee colour. Stir in the fruit, peel and nuts. Dust the tart cases with icing sugar. Spoon in the warm nut mixture and leave to set.

HONEY AND PINE NUT TARTS

115g caster sugar
115g unsalted butter, diced
3 eggs, beaten
175g flower honey
115g plain flour
Zest of 1 lemon
225g pine nuts
Pinch of salt
About 20 4 cm tart shells
Icing sugar

Whip the butter and sugar until light and fluffy. Stir in the pine nuts and the eggs one at a time. Fold in the honey, flour, lemon zest and salt. Spoon into the tart shells and bake for about 30 minutes in a preheated 185C oven. Delicious with caramelised figs.

APPLE TARTS WITH HAZELNUT PASTRY

Hazelnut pastry - substitute hazelnuts
    for the walnuts in the walnut pastry
    recipe
4 cooking apples, peeled, cored and
    finely diced
2 pears, peeled, cored and finely diced
50g sultanas
60g light brown sugar
1 tsp ground cinnamon
2 tsp cornflour

Combine the apples, pears, sultanas, sugar, cinnamon and cornflour and fill the hazelnut pastry tarts and bake.

MANGO AND COCONUT TARTS

100g butter
40g coconut flour
½ cup icing sugar
¼ cup shaved coconut plus extra
2 egg whites
1 mango, ½ diced and ½ sliced
Coconut rum or regular rum
Soft whipped cream to serve
Butter puff tart cases

Melt the butter in a saucepan and cook until golden. Put the coconut flour, icing sugar, ¼ cup shaved coconut and the strained butter into a food processor. Add the egg whites and blend well to reduce the size of the coconut. When finished mixing, add a small quantity of the shredded coconut to give some texture. Refrigerate overnight. Preheat the oven to 180C. Combine some of the mixture with a little diced mango. Spoon into butter puff pastry cases or spoon directly into greased patty tins and arrange slices of mango on top. Bake for about 20 minutes or until cooked. Serve with soft whipped cream which has a little coconut rum or regular rum added.
Makes about 4 x 9 cm tarts.

MACADAMIA LIME TARTS

125g butter, chopped
125g plain flour
60g icing sugar
60g butter, melted
1 egg
100g brown sugar
Lime, juice and zest
100g macadamia nuts, chopped
Icing sugar to serve

Process the chopped butter, flour and icing sugar in a food processor until smooth. Bring the dough together and knead gently on a floured board then roll teaspoonsful of mixture into balls and press into base and half way up the sides of mini tins. Refrigerate for about 30 minutes. Combine melted butter, egg, sugar and lime zest and juice in a bowl and mix until smooth. Sprinkle each tart with macadamia nuts and spoon lime mixture over. Bake at 170C for about 20 minutes until golden. Cool in the tin. Sprinkle with icing sugar to serve. **Makes 36.**

PINE NUT CLUSTERS

50g caster sugar
25g butter
1 tsp liquid glucose
1 tsp water
100g pine nuts, toasted

Put the sugar in a saucepan and over a medium heat cook to a light caramel. Carefully add the butter, glucose and water and mix gently until smooth. Stir in the pine nuts and cook for 30 seconds. Mix well then drop small spoonfuls of the mixture onto a parchment paper lined tray. Leave to cool to set.

WALNUT PASTRY TARTS WITH MASCARPONE, POACHED QUINCE AND HONEY WALNUTS

Walnut pastry

225g (1 ½ cups) plain flour
125g butter
2 tbsp caster sugar
1 ¼ cups finely chopped walnuts
1 egg beaten
1 tsp vanilla
Mascarpone for filling

Mix the flour, butter, sugar and walnuts until it resembles breadcrumbs. Add the egg and vanilla. Turn the dough onto a lightly floured surface and knead gently. Wrap in clingfilm and chill for at least an hour. Roll out and line the chosen size of tart tins. Refrigerate again for 30 minutes. Line with parchment paper and add baking beads. Bake in a preheated 190C oven for 15-20 minutes. Remove the beads and paper and return to the oven until the crust is golden. Fill with the Mascarpone, poached quince and honey walnuts.

Variation

This pastry is also delicious filled with lemon or orange curd.

Poached quince

2 large quinces, peeled and finely diced
1 cup sugar
Squeeze of lemon juice

Cover the diced quince in a saucepan, add the sugar and lemon juice and enough water to cover the fruit. Gently poach the quince until just cooked. Cool in the liquid. When cool reduce the liquid to a sugary syrup.

Honey walnuts

1 tsp butter
1 tsp honey
Walnut pieces

Heat the butter and the honey in a small frying pan until it foams and starts to caramelise. Toss in the walnuts and coat. Turn out onto baking parchment and separate the walnuts to cool.

CRUMBLE TOPPED MASCARPONE AND PLUM TARTS

1 cup muesli
¼ cup mixed nuts such as almonds, pecans, pistachios
¼ cup brown sugar
50g butter
Mascarpone or Philadelphia cream cheese
Plums
Ready made pastry cases or make almond pastry cases

Pulse the muesli, nuts and sugar and add the butter. Pipe a small amount of Mascarpone in the base of the tart cases and top with slices of plum. Cover with the crumble mix. Bake in a 180C oven until golden.

Variation

Fill with nectarine and caramel sauce (170g butter, 255g sugar and 20ml Armagnac, gently simmered till thick). Top with the crumble mix.

TAMARILLO UPSIDE DOWN CAKES

50g butter
½ cup brown sugar
6 tamarillos, peeled and cut
    into 2cm slices
300g butter, softened
½ cup caster sugar
½ cup brown sugar, firmly packed
3 eggs, separated
1 tsp vanilla essence
1 ½ cups self raising flour
Pinch salt
½ tsp each ground cinnamon,
    nutmeg, ground ginger
1 cup pecan nuts, finely chopped

Melt the first measure of butter and pour over the base of mini muffin tins. Sprinkle the first measure of brown sugar over the butter. Arrange the tamarillo slices on top of the sugar. Cream the butter and sugars. Add the egg yolks, one at a time, beating well. Add the vanilla. Sift in the flour, salt and spices. Add the nuts and fold to combine. In a separate bowl, beat the egg whites to soft peaks. Gently fold into the mixture. Spoon over the fruit. Bake for about 40 minutes. Stand for 10 minutes before turning out. Serve warm, dusted with icing sugar.

PISTACHIOS AND ROSE WATER SYRUP MASCARPONE IN BRIK PASTRY CUPS

6 sheets of brik pastry or
    1 packet filo pastry
½ cup butter, melted
½ cup white sugar
1 cup water
1 ½ tbsp rose water
50ml lemon juice
200g Mascarpone
150g pistachio nuts, crushed or slivers
Figs to garnish

Firstly make the pastry cases by brushing the filo or brik pastry with the melted butter with a drop or two of rose water added. Working quickly cut into 6cm rounds and mould into mini muffin tins. Hold into place with baking beads and bake for about 10 minutes in a moderate oven or until lightly golden. For the syrup, add a little water with the sugar and caramelise in a thick based pan by placing over medium heat. Do not stir. When golden, but not burnt, remove from the heat and add the cup of water taking great care as the mixture will steam. Return to the heat and boil on a high heat until thick again. Remove from the heat and add the rose water and lemon juice. Chill before using. Mix the Mascarpone with the pistachios and 2 tbsp of the syrup and chill. When ready to assemble spoon the chilled Mascarpone mixture into the cups and garnish with a slice of fig and drizzle with a little extra syrup.

LEMON CURD OR COCONUT AND LIME CURD FILLED ANISEED PASTRY TARTS

Aniseed pastry
200g plain flour
120g butter, chilled
60g icing sugar
2 tsp aniseed
1 egg yolk
2 tbsp Sambuca

Process the flour, butter and icing sugar in a food processor until the mixture resembles breadcrumbs. Add the aniseed, egg and Sambuca and pulse to bring the mixture together. Wrap the mixture in clingfilm and refrigerate for a couple of hours before rolling out and using. **Makes 40-45 4 ½ cm tarts.**

Lemon curd
125g butter
225g sugar
3 eggs
Zest and juice of 2 lemons or 3 limes
Berries to garnish

Melt the butter in the top part of a double saucepan, placed over low heat. Add the sugar slowly and stir until well blended. Beat the eggs and pour them gradually into the butter and sugar mixture. Stir until light and creamy. Do not allow the mixture to get too hot. Add the zest to the mixture then the strained juice. Add slowly, stirring all the time. Over low heat, stir until the curd forms and a film forms on the back of a spoon. Pour into screw top jars until ready to use.

Coconut and lime curd
100g unsalted butter
1 cup caster sugar
1 tbsp finely grated lime rind
⅓ cup fresh lime juice, strained
3 eggs, lightly whisked
½ cup desiccated coconut

Prepare the curd as above and add the coconut towards the end.

PETITE RICOTTA AND PEACH CAKES

½ cup Ricotta
1 cup caster sugar
1 egg
100ml milk
100ml vegetable oil
Zest of half an orange
1 cup self raising flour
6 peaches, poached
Icing sugar to serve

Blend together the Ricotta, sugar, egg, milk, oil and the orange zest. Fold in the flour. Place the mixture into the base of mini muffin tins. Top with the sliced poached peaches. Bake at 170C for about 15 minutes. Sprinkle with icing sugar to serve.

SEMOLINA TARTS FILLED WITH FINGER LIME CURD

¼ cup fine semolina
1 cup milk
1 tbsp maple syrup
1 tbsp lemon zest
Finger lime curd to fill
Finger lime flesh to garnish

Toast the semolina in a saucepan for a few minutes. Separately heat the milk with the maple syrup then slowly add the milk to the semolina, whisking constantly. On a gentle heat whisk for about 5 minutes. The mixture should be thick. Fold in the zest. Roll into a log and wrap in parchment paper. Allow to cool slightly then slice into 1cm rounds. Make a dent in the centre. Bake at 180C for about 15 minutes until they change colour. Allow to cool. When ready to serve fill with finger lime curd, and garnish with the finger lime beads.

TREACLE TARTS

Shortcrust pastry
1 cup maple or golden syrup
3 tbsp ground almonds
½ tsp finely grated lemon rind
2 tsp lemon juice
1 ½ tbsp beaten egg
3 tbsp double cream
40g fresh breadcrumbs

Roll out the pastry and line the tart tins and chill until required. For the filling combine all the ingredients and spoon into the pastry case. Bake in a preheated oven at 190C for about 15 minutes until risen and golden brown. Cool slightly before turning out. Serve fresh.

STICKY RICE CUBES WITH SHAVED COCONUT AND DRAGON FRUIT

20g black glutinous rice,
    soaked for several hours
100g arborio rice, rinsed
80g palm sugar
400ml coconut milk
Splash of coconut rum (optional)
10g shaved coconut, chopped
    plus extra for garnish
Dried pineapple to garnish
Dried dragon fruit to garnish

Cover the black rice with water and simmer for about 10 mins. Drain and rinse to remove some of the colour. Heat the coconut milk, add the palm sugar and dissolve. Add the rum, black and white rice and shaved coconut. Transfer to an ovenproof dish and bake covered for about 30 minutes until all the liquid has been absorbed and the rice is soft. Allow to cool then mould into a cube or spread on a tray to about 2 ½ cm depth. Allow to cool completely to set then cut into desired shape and size. Garnish with dried pineapple, dried dragon fruit and shaved coconut.
Makes about 16 3cm cubes.

CHRISTMAS MINCEMEAT BON BONS

Filo pastry
2 tbsp butter, melted
1 jar luxury Christmas mincemeat
Icing sugar for dusting

Cut the filo sheets in half lengthwise and again across the width. Brush each sheet with butter and place a teaspoon of mincemeat in the centre at the top. Roll and squeeze at both ends to form a bon bon shape. Bake in a moderately hot oven until golden. Dust with icing sugar when cold.

GREEN TEA AND MINT ICE CREAM ON TAPIOCA PEARLS AND ROSE WATER

1 packet Japanese green tea
    ice cream mix
Handful of fresh mint leaves
175ml full cream milk
100ml cream
Tapioca pearls, soaked in water
    for 3 hours then cooked in
    boiling water
1 tbsp sugar
Few drops of rose water
Dried rose petals
A few drops of Grenadine for colour
Mint leaves to garnish
Dried rose buds to garnish

Bring the milk to the boil. Remove from the heat and add the mint leaves and allow to steep for a couple of hours. Remove the mint leaves. Stir in the cream and the green tea ice cream mix. Churn in an ice cream machine following the maker's instructions. Make a sugar syrup with ½ cup water and the sugar. Add a few dried rose petals and a few drops of rose water. Boil for a few minutes to form a thin syrup. Allow to cool and add the tapioca pearls. Add a couple of drops of Grenadine for colour. Assemble in glasses, top with mint tea ice cream and garnish with mint leaves and a rose bud.

SAFFRON KULFI WITH ROSE SYRUP

1 tin sweetened condensed milk
720ml fresh cream, lightly whipped
1 heaped tsp freshly ground green
    cardamom seeds
1 ½g saffron threads, soaked
    in 1 tbsp warm milk
Rose syrup

Gently mix the condensed milk and the lightly whipped cream. Do not whisk. Add the cardamom seeds and saffron threads to the milk and mix gently. Pour the mixture into moulds and place them in the freezer for 4-6 hours or until set. Turn out and serve with rose syrup.

Rose syrup
¼ cup sugar
¼ cup rose water
2 tbsp sherry

Boil the sugar and rose water together and add the sherry.

DANISH APPLE AEBLESKIVER

4g dry instant yeast
200ml lukewarm milk
150g plain flour
½ tsp ground cardamom
½ tsp vanilla extract
2 tbsp caster sugar
1 egg, separated
1 apple or pear, cut into small dices
1 tbsp butter, melted
Vegetable oil
Icing sugar and raspberry jam to serve
1 aebleskiver pan*

Dissolve the yeast in the milk in a large bowl and add the butter. In a separate bowl sift together the flour, cardamom and ½ tsp salt. Add the vanilla seeds and sugar. Whisk the egg yolks into the milk. Add the dry ingredients and mix into a dough. Whisk the egg whites until stiff and fold into the dough. Stand the mixture for an hour. Oil then heat the aebleskiver pan in a 190C oven. Pour in the batter and top each with a cube of apple or pear. Cook for about 5-7 minutes or until golden. Remove from the pan and dust with icing sugar. These are also excellent cooked without the apple or pear and cut in half after cooking and filled with raspberry jam. **Makes about 30 mini aebleshiver.**

*Similar to a Japanese takoyaki pan or an old fashioned gem scone pan.

TUILES

7 egg whites
200g icing sugar
150g plain flour
200g butter, melted

Mix the ingredients well and refrigerate for at least 4 hours. Heat the oven to 180C. Spoon a small amount of the batter on a parchment lined baking tray spreading the mixture as thinly and evenly as possible. The mixture spreads, so cook only two at a time. Bake for about 8-10 minutes. When still warm shape into a desired shape - cone, cup or roll. Serve with berries and ice cream or lemon curd.

COCONUT WAFERS

1 ½ tbsp caster sugar
1 ½ tbsp honey
1 tsp lemon juice
1 tbsp coconut flour
1 tbsp shredded coconut
1 tbsp coconut cream

Mix all the ingredients together. Place small spoonfuls of the mixture onto a parchment lined baking tray making sure the wafers are well spaced as the mixture will spread. Bake in a 150C oven for about 10 minutes, or until the wafers are set. Remove gently and cool on a rack. These go well with mango mousse or any other tropical mousse. **Makes 8.**

JASMINE TEA GANACHE FILLED CHOCOLATE POTS WITH SPICED PINEAPPLE

1 cup whipping cream
2 sachets of jasmine tea
Pinch of nutmeg
80g dark bitter chocolate
    (or replace 30g with milk
    chocolate)
Chocolate pots
Mint leaves to garnish

Bring the cream, nutmeg and tea to the boil. Remove from the heat and allow to infuse for about 15 minutes. Remove the tea and whisk in the chocolate little by little. Pour into the chocolate pots and garnish with the spiced pineapple and mint leaves. Allow to set before serving - several hours.

Spiced pineapple
2 very thin slices of pineapple
Sprinkling of five spice powder

Sprinkle the pineapple with the five spice powder and dry out in a dehydrator or place on a rack and dry out in a 60C oven for about 6-8 hours.

COCONUT SAMOSAS

5 tbsp milk
50g caster sugar
50g desiccated coconut
50g sultanas, roughly chopped
½ tsp crushed cardamom seeds
2 ½ sheets filo pastry or brik pastry
40g butter, melted

Put the milk, sugar and coconut in a saucepan and cook over a gentle heat until all the liquid has been absorbed. Add the sultanas and cardamom seeds and leave to become cold. Cut each sheet of filo into eight strips about 5cm wide and brush each one with melted butter. Place a teaspoon of mixture at one end and roll into a triangle. Place on a parchment lined baking tray, brush with the remaining melted butter and bake in a preheated 190C oven for about 10 minutes until crisp and golden. Serve warm.

SWEET OVEN PANCAKES

½ cup milk
3 eggs
½ cup plain flour
Pinch of salt
½ tsp vanilla
40ml butter, melted
Icing sugar for dusting
Berries, lemon curd, jam or
    cream for topping

Preheat the oven to 200C. Grease mini muffin tins and heat before filling. Blend all the ingredients well and half fill the muffin tins. Bake for about 15 minutes or until puffed and golden. Allow to cool and dust with icing sugar. Top with mixed berries, lemon curd and blueberries or berry jam and cream.

TAPIOCA PEARLS TOPPED WITH AMARULA CREAM

¼ cup tapioca pearls, soaked in
    water for 3 hours
1 tbsp Camp coffee (coffee essence)
¾ cup full cream milk
1 tbsp sugar, or to taste
Amarula cream liqueur for topping
⅓ cup full cream milk for foam

Cook the tapioca pearls by boiling in a large pot of water. Stir during cooking. Rinse in cold water after cooking. Bring the Camp coffee, milk and sugar to the boil and simmer for a few minutes. Remove from the heat. Add the cooked tapioca pearls and cool a little before pouring into the glasses. Add a layer of Amarula cream liqueur then finally top with foam made with a milk frother if you have one.

CAPPUCCINO BRÛLÉE

Brûlée

5 medium egg yolks
75g caster sugar
230ml double cream
230ml milk
15g coffee essence
15g instant coffee

Whisk together the egg yolks and the sugar. In a saucepan mix the cream and milk with the coffee and bring to the boil. Add to the egg mixture and stir well. Pass through a fine strainer into 8 demitasse cups, or tea cups, to half way up the side. Seal each cup with a piece of foil and place into a bain-marie. Fill the dish to half way up the sides of the cups. Bake for 40-50 minutes or until the brûlées are firm. Remove the cups from the bain-marie and allow to cool.

Cream topping

150ml milk
30g caster sugar
1 medium egg yolk
10g flour
10g cornflour
250ml double cream, semi whipped
8 tbsp demerara sugar
Few drops of vanilla essence
Chocolate coated coffee beans, optional

Bring the milk to the boil with the vanilla. Mix together the sugar and egg yolk, then stir in the flour and cornflour. Pour the boiling milk onto the egg mixture and whisk together. Return to the pan over a low heat for one minute, stirring constantly until it thickens. Pour the mixture quickly into a food processor and process until smooth. Transfer to a bowl and cover with clingfilm so that it touches the cream to prevent a skin forming. When cold fold in the semi whipped cream. Spoon the pastry cream about 2 cm thick onto each brûlée, using the back of the spoon to smooth it. Sprinkle a thin layer of brown sugar on each, then caramelise with a blow torch. Stand the cups on their saucers and serve. Garnish with chocolate coated coffee beans.

Index

First published in 2014 by Gillian Flower
www.spicedlemon.com

The moral right of the author has been asserted.

Copyright © 2014 in text: Gillian Flower
Copyright © 2014 in photographs: Gillian Flower, Drew Joyce, Trevor Newman and Robert Sampson
Copyright © 2014: SpicedLemon Catering

Design: Trevor Newman
Contributing Editor: Di Buckley

ISBN: 978-0-646-92536-3

Printed through Benefitz New Zealand